Life During the Roman Empire

Stuart A. Kallen

ReferencePoint
Press®

San Diego, CA

© 2014 ReferencePoint Press, Inc.
Printed in the United States

For more information, contact:
ReferencePoint Press, Inc.
PO Box 27779
San Diego, CA 92198
www. ReferencePointPress.com

LIBRARY OF CONGRESS CATALOGING-IN-PUBLICATION DATA

Kallen, Stuart A., 1955-
  Life during the Roman Empire / by Stuart A. Kallen.
    pages cm. -- (Living history series)
  Includes bibliographical references and index.
  ISBN-13: 978-1-60152-570-3 (hardback)
  ISBN-10: 1-60152-570-2 (hardback)
  1. Rome--Social life and customs--Juvenile literature. 2. Rome--Civilization--Juvenile literature. I. Title.
  DG78.K35 2013
  937'.06--dc23
                                                                      2012044980

Contents

Foreword   4

Important Events of the Roman Empire   6

Introduction   8
  A Vibrant Society

Chapter One   12
  Home and Family

Chapter Two   26
  Working for a Living

Chapter Three   40
  Life as a Legionnaire

Chapter Four   56
  Leisure and Entertainment

Chapter Five   69
  Worshipping the Gods and Spirits

Source Notes   84

For Further Research   88

Index   90

Picture Credits   95

About the Author   96

Foreword

History is a complex and multifaceted discipline that embraces many different areas of human activity. Given the expansive possibilities for the study of history, it is significant that since the advent of formal writing in the Ancient Near East over six thousand years ago, the contents of most nonfiction historical literature have been overwhelmingly limited to politics, religion, warfare, and diplomacy.

Beginning in the 1960s, however, the focus of many historical works experienced a substantive change worldwide. This change resulted from the efforts and influence of an ever-increasing number of progressive contemporary historians who were entering the halls of academia. This new breed of academician, soon accompanied by many popular writers, argued for a major revision of the study of history, one in which the past would be presented from the ground up. What this meant was that the needs, wants, and thinking of ordinary people should and would become an integral part of the human record. As British historian Mary Fulbrook wrote in her 2005 book, *The People's State: East German Society from Hitler to Honecker*, students should be able to view "history with the people put back in." This approach to understanding the lives and times of people of the past has come to be known as social history. According to contemporary social historians, national and international affairs should be viewed not only from the perspective of those empowered to create policy but also through the eyes of those over whom power is exercised.

The American historian and best-selling author, Louis "Studs" Terkel, was one of the pioneers in the field of social history. He is best remembered for his oral histories, which were firsthand accounts of everyday life drawn from the recollections of interviewees who lived during pivotal events or periods in history. Terkel's first book, *Division Street America* (published in 1967), focuses on urban living in and around Chicago and is a compilation of seventy interviews of immigrants and native-born Americans. It was followed by several other oral histories including *Hard Times* (the 1930s depression), *Working* (people's feelings about their jobs), and his 1985 Pulitzer Prize–winning *The Good War* (about life in America before, during, and after World War II).

In keeping with contemporary efforts to present history by people and about people, ReferencePoint's *Living History* series offers students a journey through recorded history as recounted by those who lived it. While modern sources such as those found in *The Good War* and on radio and TV interviews are readily available, those dating to earlier periods in history are scarcer and often more obscure the further back in time one investigates. These important primary sources are there nonetheless waiting to be discovered in literary formats such as posters, letters, and diaries, and in artifacts such as vases, coins, and tombstones. And they are also found in places as varied as ancient Mesopotamia, Charles Dickens's England, and Nazi concentration camps. The *Living History* series uncovers these and other available sources as they relate the "living history" of real people to their student readers.

Important Events

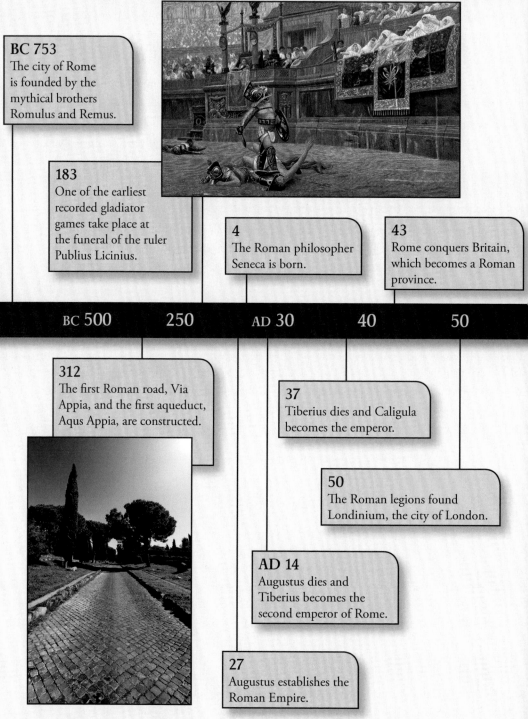

BC 753
The city of Rome is founded by the mythical brothers Romulus and Remus.

183
One of the earliest recorded gladiator games take place at the funeral of the ruler Publius Licinius.

4
The Roman philosopher Seneca is born.

43
Rome conquers Britain, which becomes a Roman province.

BC **500**   **250**   AD **30**   **40**   **50**

312
The first Roman road, Via Appia, and the first aqueduct, Aqus Appia, are constructed.

37
Tiberius dies and Caligula becomes the emperor.

50
The Roman legions found Londinium, the city of London.

AD 14
Augustus dies and Tiberius becomes the second emperor of Rome.

27
Augustus establishes the Roman Empire.

of the Roman Empire

64
The Great Fire of Rome burns for nine days and destroys two-thirds of the city.

79
Mount Vesuvius erupts and destroys the Italian city of Pompeii.

121
Construction begins on Hadrian's Wall in the north of England.

476
The western Roman empire collapses.

100   200   300   400   500

104
Trajan's Baths are constructed in Rome.

212
Emperor Caracalla issues an edict granting full citizenship to all free men and women in the Roman Empire.

390
Military expert Flavius Vegetius writes the Roman legion manual *On Military Matters*.

98
The Roman Empire reaches its greatest expanse.

70
Construction begins on the Roman Colosseum.

Introduction

A Vibrant Society

In 27 BC, when Augustus became the first emperor of the Roman Empire, ushering in the imperial era, the nation he ruled was already more than seven hundred years old. For centuries, Rome's rulers had controlled a vast territory that extended into northern Europe and parts of Africa and Asia. The city of Rome, the capital, was one of the most beautiful and sophisticated in the world. It was filled with parks and gardens, marble arches and statues, luxurious palaces, huge amphitheaters, and sprawling universities. All were linked by a complex network of roads and water-bearing aqueducts. As the capital of the most powerful nation on earth, Rome was a center of world culture.

By AD 98, imperial Rome reached its maximum size, becoming the largest empire in history. The vast empire contained about 60 million people, or approximately one-quarter of Earth's population. Romans, who spoke Latin, referred to their lands as the *imperium sine fine*, or "empire without end." The empire stretched through the modern nations of Spain, France, England, Netherlands, and Germany. It encompassed much of eastern Europe, including Slovenia, Romania, Armenia, and Croatia. The empire without end spread across North Africa from Morocco to Egypt and east into Turkey, Syria, and Iraq. All the territories were united under Roman rule, as Italian scientist Alberto Angela explains: "Everywhere the official language was Latin. Everywhere, payments were made in sestertii [brass Roman coins]. Everywhere, there was only one law: Roman law."[1]

Towns and Cities

The majority of Roman subjects lived in isolated tribal communities where life had changed little in thousands of years. Rural Romans hunted, fished, grew meager crops, and tended livestock. During the imperial era London and Paris were little more than small military outposts with fewer than 8,000 people. Many of the residents were Roman soldiers called legionnaires. However, the empire also encompassed the era's most developed and cultured cities. About 500,000 people lived in Alexandria, Egypt, with a similar number in Carthage, in what is now Tunisia. The Syrian city of Antioch, in present-day Turkey, had about 200,000 inhabitants.

Patricians, Citizens, and Slaves

The city of Rome contained a vibrant, multicultural society unlike any other. With about 1.5 million residents, Rome was, according to Angela, home to "rich matrons reclining on their couches, Greek doctors, cavalry officers from Gaul [France], Italian senators, Spanish sailors, Egyptian priests, Cypriot prostitutes, Middle Eastern merchants, German slaves."[2]

While people from various regions mixed freely on city streets, Roman society throughout the empire was strictly divided by a class structure based on wealth and whether a person was free or slave. Men, especially the father, or *pater* in Latin, were the primary authority figures in most families. Wealthy males called patricians, meaning "fathers of the state," controlled the lives of tens of millions of people throughout the empire. Several dozen patricians held most of the power and status; they were heads of large, extremely wealthy families who owned most of the land. A less wealthy but still powerful class of patricians, numbering about thirty-five thousand, controlled political and religious institutions in approximately three hundred towns and cities throughout the empire. Together the patrician class owned 80 percent of all wealth in imperial Rome.

> **WORDS IN CONTEXT**
> **patrician**
> During the Roman Empire, a man who possessed great wealth.

The next level in class structure consisted of Romans citizens known as plebeians or plebs. (An individual plebeian was called a pleb, based on the Latin word *plebis*, meaning "common person.") Plebs had a variety of

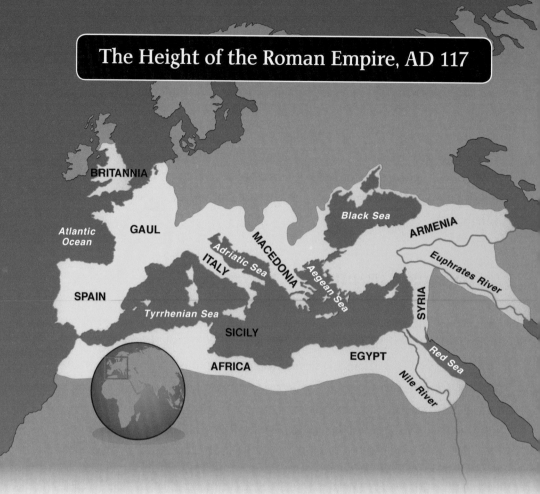

The Height of the Roman Empire, AD 117

BRITANNIA

Atlantic Ocean

GAUL

SPAIN

ITALY

Adriatic Sea

MACEDONIA

Tyrrhenian Sea

SICILY

AFRICA

Aegean Sea

Black Sea

ARMENIA

Euphrates River

SYRIA

EGYPT

Red Sea

Nile River

privileges including the right to marry, sign legal contracts, run businesses, and stand for civil office. To qualify for citizenship, a man or woman had to be born of parents who were not slaves. Plebs, regardless of gender, were called freemen.

The final division of the Roman class structure consisted of slaves. Historians believe slaves made up approximately 15 percent of the empire's population; in Italy the percentage was much higher, reaching about 35 percent. Slaves had few rights; they could be whipped, beaten, branded, sexually abused, tortured, and even castrated. Not all slaves were treated harshly—some worked as shopkeepers and administrators and lived better than average plebs. However, the typical slave who labored as a servant, miner, or farm worker in the countryside led a hopeless, degrading, and brutal existence.

Slaves had one way to escape their class. They were allowed to keep any money earned while working on their own time and to use that money to buy their freedom. Those who managed to buy their way out of slavery were known as freedmen or freedwomen. These fortunate ex-slaves were accepted by Roman society and did not face ongoing discrimination. Freedmen and freedwomen had most of the rights of other Roman citizens—and when they had children, their children were considered freemen.

> **WORDS IN CONTEXT**
> **plebs**
> Freeborn, lower- and middle-class Romans.

An Influential Civilization

Whether Romans were slaves, plebs, or patricians, their daily activities contributed to an advanced culture that influenced Western civilization long after the empire collapsed in AD 476. The deeds of Roman gladiators, legionnaires, and emperors have inspired countless books, plays, and films. The architects, builders, and masons constructed huge coliseums, marble monuments, and other structures that have long been admired. The words of the empire's philosophers, playwrights, and poets such as Virgil, Cicero, and Horace have been studied for centuries. Through their efforts, the Roman Empire reshaped the ancient world.

Chapter One

Home and Family

The Roman Empire was the most powerful and well-organized nation in the ancient world, with borders extending from the icy seas of northern England to the burning Sahara desert in Africa. Despite its strength as a military power, most Romans believed their greatest virtues could be traced to something much closer to home. The family, or *familia*, was the empire's most revered institution.

Like other aspects of Roman society, the family was organized around a strict hierarchy. In a Roman family the father, known as the *paterfamilias*, was the undisputed master of the house. Roman laws ensured that the father had absolute power over the members of his household, both family and slaves. The paterfamilias controlled all family property, acted as the family priest, and could accept or reject marriages of his sons and daughters. He could also determine what family members did for a living. The senior male expected unconditional loyalty and total respect for his authority. Those who disobeyed him could face harsh punishment. In extreme cases of disobedience, fathers could sell their children into slavery or even kill them. With this power came responsibility. The paterfamilias was responsible for the welfare of his family.

While fathers were seen as strict authorities, Roman writers often viewed their mothers as virtuous and indulgent. As the philosopher Seneca explained in the first century AD: "The father orders his children to be aroused from sleep in order that they may start early upon their pursuits,—even on holidays he does not permit them to be idle, and he draws from them sweat and sometimes tears. But the mother fondles them in her lap, wishes to keep them out of the sun, wishes them never to be unhappy, never to cry, never to toil."[3]

Short Lives

Roman families were unlike modern families, which often include people from several generations such as children, parents, grandparents, and even great-grandparents. In the Roman Empire the average life expectancy was very short due to disease, war, poor nutrition, and high rates of infant mortality. About one-quarter of babies born during this era died before their first birthdays, and another quarter died before the age of ten. Many women died during childbirth, and a host of diseases such as tuberculosis, typhoid, cholera, and smallpox killed millions.

Some wealthy patricians lived long lives. The emperor Augustus was 76 when he

died, the statesman Cato the Elder was 85. However, these cases were unusual. The average age of death for plebs was 27, and few people lived past 50. In this environment, girls were expected to marry and bear children when they were in their early teens. Marriages were arranged by families, and the bride had little say in the matter. As the first century physician Soranus of Ephesus writes, "women are married for the sake of bearing children and heirs, and not for pleasure and enjoyment."[4]

When spouses died, survivors often remarried. This created extended families that might include parents, children, stepparents, stepchildren, half-siblings, and others. The absence of government assistance forced people to depend on their large family networks for survival.

Living in the *Insulae*

If the family was the most important institution in Rome, the family home ranked a close second. According to first century BC philosopher and Roman senator Cicero: "What more sacred, what more strongly guarded by every holy feeling, than a man's own home?"[5] While Cicero lived in a lavish villa surrounded by gardens and orchards, the majority of plebs lived in cramped apartments located in multistory buildings called *insulae* (the singular form is *insula*). Most of these buildings were 50 to 70 feet (15.2 to 21 m) in height—five to seven stories—but a few

The average Roman lived in multistory, cramped apartment buildings called insulae. *Pictured is an architectural model of one such complex.*

were nine stories high. During the imperial era, the insulae were the tallest residential buildings in the world, vertical villages that acted as the skyscrapers of ancient Rome.

Like many modern apartment buildings, the insula was square in shape, built of brick, with evenly spaced rectangular windows. Many of these structures bore names, such as the Insula Felicles. A typical insula provided shelter for six or seven families, around forty people. The ground floors of insulae were used for shops, booths, and businesses. The owners of the enterprises lived in small apartments behind their stores. The second floors held large apartments occupied by wealthier tenants. These residences offered wooden balconies, glass windows, running water, and toilets.

The poorest residents of the insulae were forced to trudge up dark, narrow stairways or even climb ladders to reach the upper floors, where small apartments were densely packed. Each single-room dwelling was separated from the neighbor's by a thin wooden panel. Despite their generally large size, families usually slept in one room.

One corner of the apartment was dedicated to cooking and eating. Most plebs had fairly nutritious diets. They ate grain-based breads and porridges; vegetables such as beans, onions, cabbages, and cucumbers; and fruits, including figs, grapes, apples, and pears. Eggs, cheese, and olive oil played a major nutritional role, but meat, such as pork, veal, or poultry, was expensive and eaten only on special occasions.

Since hunger often set off peasant revolutions in the ancient world, Roman emperors provided free or very inexpensive wheat to plebs. While subsidizing grain was expensive, it helped rulers maintain power.

> **WORDS IN CONTEXT**
> *insulae*
> Multi-story, brick apartment buildings that provided homes for the vast majority of Roman plebs.

Crumbling and Burning

Upper-floor insulae apartments had no window glass, only translucent animal skins or crude shutters to keep out the wind, rain, and cold. The apartments also lacked heat, running water, and toilets. However, the city maintained 144 lavishly decorated, well-maintained public latrines, which cost a few pennies to use. The latrines were continually flushed with cascades of water flowing from the city's famous aqueducts, elevated stone waterways that brought in spring water from the hills north of Rome.

Lack of water compounded the fire dangers associated with living on the upper floors of the insulae. Most people cooked on coal-fired grills and lit their rooms with candles, torches, and smoky oil lamps. Fires were frequent, and those living on the lowest floors had the best chance for escape. In the late first century the Roman author Juvenal wrote about a fire in an insulae: "Ucalegon [a third-floor resident] is already shouting for water and shifting his [belongings]; smoke is pouring out of your third-floor attic above, but you [who live above] know nothing of it; for if the alarm begins on the ground-floor, the last man to burn will be he who has nothing to shelter him from the rain but the [roof] tiles, where the gentle doves lay their eggs."[6]

In many parts of Rome the insulae were packed so closely together that a fire in one building quickly spread to the others. This was a regular occurrence, and on occasion entire city blocks were leveled by flames and hundreds of people were killed. In AD 64, for example, the Great Fire of Rome burned for nine days and left two-thirds of the city a smoldering ruin.

With fires regularly consuming insulae, contractors constructed them as cheaply as possible, assuming the buildings would likely burn to the ground within a few years. The apartments were notorious for crumbling and collapsing on their tenants. Once again, Juvenal sums up the situation: "But here we inhabit a city supported for the most part by slender props; for that is how the [landlord] holds up the tottering house, patches up gaping cracks in the old wall, bidding the inmates sleep at ease under a roof ready to crumble about their ears."[7]

The Roman poet Catullus was so afraid of his apartment disintegrating or burning that he derisively writes that homeless "beggars were fortunate in not having to fear either."[8]

Domestic Life in the *Domūs*

Life was quite different for the patrician who lived in a *domus* (plural form is *domūs*), Latin for "house," from which the word *domestic* is derived. Insulae far outnumbered domūs in Rome. According to a fourth century survey, there was only one domus for every twenty-six blocks of insulae in the city.

Domūs all shared certain features. A typical domus was one or two stories high and built like a small fortress, with a windowless brick wall facing the chaos of the street. In the wall, a set of double doors with a large bronze doorknocker and doorknobs provided access to the residence. Inside, slaves were stationed to protect the entrance from burglars and chase away door-to-door solicitors who were a problem even in the time of emperors.

Beyond the walls the domus had several features. The *vestibulum*, meaning "vestibule," was the main hallway that led from the entrance to

> **WORDS IN CONTEXT**
> *domus*
> A luxurious home occupied by a patrician.

In Their Own Words

The Great Fire of Rome

In AD July 64, the Great Fire of Rome broke out in the shops lining Circus Maximus, the city's huge chariot-racing stadium. Forty-five years after the tragedy, the historian Tacitus wrote a detailed account of the fire, excerpted below:

[The fire] had its beginning in that part of the circus which adjoins the Palatine and Caelian hills, where, amid the shops containing inflammable wares, the conflagration both broke out and instantly became so fierce and so rapid from the wind that it seized in its grasp the entire length of the circus. For here there were no houses fenced in by solid masonry, or temples surrounded by walls, or any other obstacle to interpose delay. The blaze in its fury ran first through the level portions of the city, then rising to the hills, while it again devastated every place below them, it outstripped all preventive measures; so rapid was the mischief and so completely at its mercy the city, with those narrow winding passages and irregular streets, which characterized old Rome. Added to this were the wailings of terror-stricken women, the feebleness of age, the helpless inexperience of childhood, the crowds who sought to save themselves or others, dragging out the infirm or waiting for them, and by their hurry in the one case, by their delay in the other, aggravating the confusion. Often, while they looked behind them, they were intercepted by flames on their side or in their face.

Tacitus, "The Annals, Book XV," trans. Alfred John Church and William Jackson Brodribb, Internet Classics Archive, March 14, 2011. http://classics.mit.edu.

the most important part of the house, the atrium. This large square room was the main living area, in which the plaster walls were decorated with brightly colored paintings called frescoes.

While the edges of the atrium were covered by a high ceiling, at the center an open-air courtyard, called a peristyle, allowed light into the domus. The roof of the atrium was constructed to channel rainwater into a shallow, rectangular sunken pool, called an *impluvium*, located at the center of the peristyle. The pool was decorative, reflecting the blue sky and clouds, but it was also practical. Rainwater from the impluvium could be piped into an underground marble well, or cistern, where it was stored for drinking, washing, and cleaning. The wealthiest domus owner might have a private water main bringing in fresh water from a nearby aqueduct, although this was rare.

Other rooms in the domus were similar to those found in contemporary homes. The *cubiculum*, or bedroom, featured a bed so high that a stool was necessary for climbing into it. The mattress would be stuffed with either straw or wool, while the sculpted bed frame might be decorated with bronze and ivory carvings of cats or mythical creatures such as half-man, half-goat satyrs.

Reality and Illusion

Most domūs featured a room off the atrium called a *tablinum*, used to conduct business. This home office and reception area might be decorated with a large, ornate desk holding a candelabra, decorative art pieces, and silver pens. Some homes also contained libraries and large meeting rooms called basilicas. Commenting on the necessity of these features in the domūs of important officials, the architect Vitruvius wrote in 35 BC: "Distinguished men, required to fulfill their duty by holding public office, must build lofty vestibules in regal style, with spacious atria and peristyles . . . also libraries and basilicas comparable with magnificent public buildings, because public meetings and private trials take place inside their houses."[9]

A modern-day visitor to a domus would notice that Romans did not much care for furniture. The walls were amply decorated with artwork and the floors with elaborate mosaics, images created with small pieces of colored glass, stone, and tile. But the rooms were not cluttered with bookshelves, couches, armchairs, and tables, as Alberto Angela explains:

> Instead of focusing attention on furniture and the room décor, [the Romans] usually try to hide them or camouflage them. Beds and chairs sometimes disappear under cushions or drapes. While at the same time, the frescoes on the walls frequently reproduce false doors, fake curtains, and fake landscapes—which might even alternate with real openings in the wall with views of the garden. . . . So, a lot of noble houses display this strange predilection of the Romans: to play hide and seek between reality and illusion.[10]

Convivial Dining

Every domus featured a *culina*, or kitchen, but family members rarely entered this room. The kitchen was the exclusive domain of slaves who prepared meals for their masters. With little attention given to decorations, kitchens were often small and dark, and the walls were blackened by smoke from cooking fires because they lacked chimneys.

While Roman plebs ate simple meals for dinner, food was extremely important to patricians who have long been celebrated for throwing lavish banquets. Their extravagant meals, called *convivia*, or convivial banquets, were held on a regular basis in the *triclinium*, or dining room. A typical triclinium was equipped with low tables and three long, embroidered couches placed in a U-shaped arrangement on thick rugs. The host sat at the center where he could direct the festivities, ordering the costume-wearing slaves to bring the next course or pour more wine.

A convivial dinner was attended by nine to twelve men and women. Although most patricians had political or financial power, it was considered inappropriate to talk business at convivia. Conversations usually centered on jokes, gossip, and war stories. In addition, professional actors, poets, or storytellers were hired to entertain the guests.

Food and wine flowed freely at lavish banquets held by the Roman Empire's wealthiest citizens. A nineteenth-century painting depicts one such banquet, which also features a performance by gladiators.

At convivia, patricians ignored the many formal social rules that governed everyday life. Wine flowed freely, and etiquette dictated that the diners eat while reclining on one side. In this relaxed posture, each diner was propped up on the left elbow, holding a plate in the hand while bringing the food to the mouth with the fingers of the right hand. (Romans did not eat with forks, but their food was cut into bite-sized pieces by slaves.) No one cared if food dropped onto clothing, and remnants such as bones, lobster shells, and fruit pits were thrown on the floor or under the couches.

Meals, which lasted six to nine hours, featured rare and expensive delicacies made from flamingos, lamprey eels, thrush tongues, and fat little rodents called dormice. Roman hosts polished their reputations by serving their guests foods that appeared to be one thing but were actually something else. The author Petronius describes the convivium held by a wealthy man named Trimalchios, whose cook created a pork dish shaped to appear as a fat goose. This was garnished with fish made from sow's organs and pigeons fashioned from bacon. Trimalchios also treated his guests to a baked boar. The boar appeared to be suckling piglets but these were actually made of cake. The cake piglets were put aside for guests to take home as gifts. In another surprise, according to Petronius, there appeared "a great bearded giant, with bands around his legs, and wearing a short hunting cape in which a design was woven. Drawing his hunting-knife, [he] plunged it fiercely into the boar's side, and some live thrushes flew out of the gash. Fowlers, ready with their rods, caught them in a moment, as they fluttered around the room."[11]

During such spectacles, belching was appreciated by hosts and even considered a sign of nobility. And on occasion, when guests ate or drank too much, it was not considered rude to drool or vomit. As Seneca explains, "When we recline at a banquet, one [slave] wipes up the spittle; another, situated beneath [the table], collects the leavings of the drunks."[12]

> **WORDS IN CONTEXT**
> *convivium*
> A long, extravagant dinner party held by a wealthy Roman.

The Practical Tunic

Beyond their unique dining habits, patricians distinguished themselves from plebs by their manner of dress. While Roman males of every class wore two types of garments, a tunic and a toga, the garments were designed to reveal the wearer's social status. The tunic closely resembled a long T-shirt of beige Egyptian linen or white wool. It was slipped over the head and fastened around the body with a belt. Tunics worn by plebs hung to the knees in front and were a little longer in back. It was a simple and practical garment, worn as a night shirt, an undergarment for a toga, or alone.

The tunics of the patricians were of different design. A patrician class of Roman businessmen, called equestrians, wore tunics that were shorter, cut just above the knee. Tunics worn by government officials, called senators, had broad, vertical purple stripes meant to indicate the man's honorable status. Men's tunics had short sleeves that only covered the top of the arm; it was considered unmanly for sleeves to be longer. According to second century author Aulus Gellius, "It was inappropriate in Rome and in all of [the Empire] for men to wear tunics stretching beyond the arms."[13] While a man's arms were to remain exposed, in cold weather he might wear two tunics. Cloaks made of Italian wool or woolen body warmers called *ventrales* were wrapped around the chest in cold weather.

Women's tunics, called *stolae,* were not as indicative of social status. They had long sleeves and were held fast by two belts. Stolae were cut at various lengths; most fell well below the knee and some extended to the feet.

The Toga

No successful senator or equestrian would be seen in public without his toga. This woolen or linen sheet, cut in a semicircle around 20 feet (6 m) wide, was comparable to a modern suit and tie and worn at all important engagements.

Putting on a huge toga required the help of a slave. While the master stood still, his slave laid one end of the huge sheet over the man's shoulders. The cloth was then passed under the right arm, pulled across the chest, and over the left shoulder. After it was fixed with a pin, about one-third of the sheet remained. This was wrapped around the body and tucked under the first layers. The wearer then had to bend his left arm at the elbow as if he was holding a drink, and the remaining cloth was draped over the forearm. For the rest of the day, the forearm remained in this position so the toga did not drag on the ground. Because of this the garment was useless for running, climbing stairs, or even sitting down comfortably.

> **WORDS IN CONTEXT**
>
> **equestrian**
>
> A class of Roman male who worked with money; included businessmen, tax collectors, and bankers.

Foreigners, slaves, and former slaves were banned from wearing togas, and most plebs did not own one. Those who did wear the garment were governed by rigid rules of dress. Average patricians wore the toga pura, a plain, off-white garment. Senators and freeborn boys under the age of sixteen were allowed to wear a toga praetexta, a white garment with a wide purple border. A purple toga with gold thread, the toga picta, was worn by generals and emperors on special occasions, such as military victory parades. Finally, the dark toga, or toga pulla, was worn for mourning.

Looking Back

Upstairs at an Insula

Scientist, historian, and Italian television personality Alberto Angela conducts an imaginary tour up the stairs to an upper-story insula apartment in AD 115:

The steps are made of unfinished bricks. . . . There is such a shortage of space that even the landing is occupied. The entire area is crisscrossed by lines of clothes hanging on ropes and beams. The floor is cluttered with unlit braziers, broken pitchers, rags, lemon rinds, and banana peels, squashed and covered with flies. . . . We push on a half–open door. Its creaking is a curtain of sound that, as the door swings open, gradually reveals to us a bare and modest room, without the slightest decoration. The walls are painted in a uniform ocher color and there is just one table with a few stools scattered here and there. . . .

A small cabinet serves as a credenza with some bread and a chunk of cheese wrapped in a piece of cloth. The original floor plan of this apartment has been radically altered by partitions and curtains, in order to create a lot of small spaces to sublet. Pulling open the curtain, we discover a single room with the straw pallet on the floor and an unlit lantern. The wardrobe consists of some nails planted in the wall holding a straw hat and a couple of tunics. Two clay pitchers and a canvas bag of food are hanging from other nails, almost certainly to keep them out of the reach of mice and insects.

Alberto Angela, *A Day in the Life of Ancient Rome.* New York: Europa, 2010, pp. 98–99.

Women's Fashions

While men wore the toga as a badge of honor, this was not the case for women. The only Roman females to wear togas were prostitutes. Women did wear a long, rectangular shawl, called a *palla*. These brightly colored wool garments extended to the knee and, like the toga, were elaborately

A wealthy Roman woman is assisted with her makeup, hair, and clothing. Women of wealth used homemade face creams to soften their skin and makeup to enhance their looks.

folded around the body. In wet or cold weather, the extra folds of the palla could be pulled up to cover the head.

Women of all classes wore jewelry, and even plebs adorned themselves with bracelets, armlets, necklaces, and rings made from gold and silver. The fashion accessories of the wealthy included pearls and precious gems such as emeralds, garnets, and sapphires. In addition, makeup was important for the fashion conscious, and Roman women beautified themselves with painted cheeks, penciled eyebrows, and eye shadow.

Roman women also applied homemade face creams to soften their skin. In the early first century AD, the Roman poet Ovid advised women to create a moisturizer from ground barley and narcissus bulbs, powdered deer horn, honey, and eggs. According to Ovid, "Any woman who smears her face with this cosmetic will make it brighter than her mirror."[14]

In addition to using cosmetics, patrician women dyed their hair with various substances, including a nontoxic dye made from the flowers of the henna plant. However, some hair dyes were poisonous and created unintended consequences: Ovid's mistress Corinna applied an unnamed coloring which caused her hair to fall out. This prompted Ovid to write: "Didn't I tell you to stop messing around with the color of your hair? Now you have no hair left to dye! If you had left it alone, who had thicker hair than you? And when you let it down, it used to hang to your waist. . . . Now your hair has fallen out, and you alone are responsible."[15] After this incident, Corinna bought an expensive imported wig. Many of these came from Germany where blond slaves were forced to cut their hair for use by wig makers.

Like other Romans, Corinna placed great value on her appearance. She lived in a society where people were judged by their beauty, status, and place in the social hierarchy. This was true in the domūs where the rich endeavored to outdo one another, and in the one-room insulae apartments where the poor struggled daily to make ends meet.

Chapter Two

Working for a Living

In AD 100, when Rome was at its economic peak, about 85 percent of the empire's residents lived and worked on the land. From North Africa to the North Sea the empire's rural farmers and slaves produced an amazing bounty of wool, meat, grains, fruits, and vegetables on small plots of land. Little wonder that the work of farming was idealized by Roman citizens.

According to legend, the city of Rome was founded on April 21, 753 BC, by Romulus and Remus, shepherds who were twin brothers. The twins united the numerous small farming communities located on Rome's seven hills to form a single magnificent city. Even as Rome grew into the largest city in Europe over the centuries, Romans continued to think of their nation as a land of honest, hardworking farmers. Whether they lived in a crowded insula or a spacious domus, urban Romans decorated their walls with pastoral scenes featuring sheep, grapevines, and olive trees. Roman intellectuals venerated farming and described country living as the one true path to happiness. As Horace wrote in 30 BC:

> Happy the man, who, remote from business, after the manner of the ancient race of mortals, cultivates his paternal lands with his own oxen; . . . he shuns both the [courtroom] and the proud portals of citizens in power. Wherefore he either weds the lofty poplars to the mature branches of the vine . . . or he takes a prospect of the herds of his lowing cattle, wandering about in a lonely vale; or stores his honey, pressed [from the combs], in clean vessels; or shears his tender sheep.[16]

Horace's verses praising hardy Roman farmers were popular for centuries among city dwellers, who were constantly challenged by traffic, noise, pollution, and crime. Ironically, Horace himself made his living destroying the way of life he idealized. He worked as a public auctioneer, selling off the lands and personal belongings of farmers who could not pay their debts. And by the first century most small, family-owned farms had vanished, and agricultural work was principally performed by slaves.

Wealthy Landholders and Slavers

Roman farmers were once independent landholders who earned a reasonable living. However, several factors changed country life during the early years of the empire. Many farmers left the land to join the Roman legion, motivated by the belief that the military provided more economic security than agriculture. This left many farms neglected or abandoned, prompting wealthy patricians to take over large swaths of land. Roman senators and other aristocrats believed that owning land and earning wealth from rents and crops was the only respectable way to make a living. Engaging in trade or business was considered vulgar by patricians.

> **WORDS IN CONTEXT**
> **foundling**
> An unwanted infant or child abandoned by its parents.

Wealthy landlords also benefited from the growing number of people forced into slavery. Some slaves were war captives, others were foundlings—unwanted infants or children abandoned by their mothers. Bandits and pirates also provided a steady stream of slaves to the empire. As the theologian Augustine noted in the fourth century:

So great is the number in the province of Africa of those who are called in common parlance "slavers," that they practically clear the province of human beings by carrying off people to sell in places across the sea. . . . Moreover, because of this mob of slavers, a throng of predators and kidnappers is so out of control that in hordes fearsomely dressed like soldiers or wild men they swoop down on certain underpopulated rural areas screaming like banshees and forcibly drag off people whom they then sell to slave dealers.[17]

Small landholders, who had only themselves and their families to work the land, found it impossible to compete with the huge estates. Many were forced to become sharecroppers, leasing land from patricians and paying rent with a percentage of the crops. Others simply went to work for the large landholders, laboring in the fields side by side with slaves. Some freeborn farmers were so desperate they sold themselves— or their children—into slavery.

Many farmers who were forced off the land moved to Roman cities. As urban areas expanded, it became necessary to import food from great distances. Emperors understood that a hungry populous was prone to riots and revolution, and the city of Rome alone required 6 million bags of grain a year to feed its inhabitants. Cities in the eastern empire were also dependent on food imports. To meet demand, wheat was grown in Sicily, Egypt, and Britain. Olive oil and wine were produced by slaves and freeborn workers in Spain. In Africa workers built dams and canals in arid savannah regions to channel water to olive and fruit trees. In Gaul (present-day France) Romans built and operated waterwheels to grind wheat into flour. All these pursuits required backbreaking labor, as British history professor Nigel Rodgers explains: "Roman wealth created no agricultural revolution. The commonest way to increase farm production was simply to work laborers, whether free or servile, harder."[18]

> **WORDS IN CONTEXT**
>
> **sharecropper**
>
> A farmer who leased land from a patrician and paid for use of the land with a percentage of his crops.

Farm Labor

Wherever farmhands labored in the Roman empire, they worked with wood and iron hand tools such as axes, rakes, shovels, hoes, shears, sickles, and saws. The Romans also adopted farm implements from conquered lands. A type of plow with a front wheel, good for breaking up heavy soil, originated in northern France. A threshing machine used to separate grain from stalks and husks was first used in Northern Africa.

Roman Empire slaves feed wood into a basement furnace. Slaves who worked inside the homes of the empire's wealthiest citizens might have cooked, cleaned, and cared for children. Other slaves worked in gardens, on farms, in bakeries, and in other settings.

On most Roman estates, these primitive tools were wielded by slaves who were overseen by a slave or freeman who acted as a foreman. The foreman scheduled chores, resolved conflicts between workers, and ensured that the master's orders were carried out. Around AD 50 the agricultural scholar Columella provided advice to landholders about selecting a good foreman:

You should choose someone who has been hardened to agricultural work from childhood and tested by experience. . . . He should no longer be a young man, since this will detract from his authority to command since old men don't like to obey some youngster; nor should he have reached old age yet, or he will not have the stamina for work of the most strenuous kind. He should be middle-aged and fit and know about agriculture. . . . Whomever you appoint as manager, you must allocate him a woman to live with him and keep him in check and also to help him in various things.[19]

The women, called forewomen, took an active role in running an estate. The forewoman might be a foreman's wife if the couple was born free. Slaves were forbidden by law to marry, but slave couples often lived as husband and wife while running an estate.

Whether free or slave, the forewomen supervised the work of female laborers. These workers spun wool into thread, wove it into cloth on a loom, dyed it, and made it into clothing. Forewomen also managed the food supply necessary to feed teams of slaves. They purchased foods, stocked pantries, and directed the cooking crew as they prepared meals several times a day. Forewomen also ensured cows and goats were milked, barns and stables were cleaned, and livestock was properly cared for. When slaves fell ill or delivered babies, the forewoman acted as a nurse or midwife, tending to patients and keeping sickrooms clean.

Treatment of Farm Slaves

Forewomen and foremen also had to essentially act as guards to prevent escapes and rebellions, which were a constant threat. To prevent uprisings Columella recommended that slaves be worked from dawn until dusk so that they would be too tired to revolt. To prevent slaves from escaping they were often forced to wear heavy iron collars which were permanently welded around the neck. These bore tags that read "If you find this slave, he has run away. Please return him to his owner at the following address."[20] Slaves who escaped were accused of theft, "stealing" their owner's property. Those who were recaptured might be branded with a red-hot iron on the face.

If an individual slave killed his owner, all the slaves on the estate were charged with the crime of failing to protect the master. Punishment was death by crucifixion and, on occasion, hundreds of slaves were killed for a crime committed by one person. The sorrowful conditions faced by farm slaves may be summed up in the term for slave lodgings, *ergastulum*, which means "lifetime prison."

Work in the Mines

If a male farm slave failed to perform his job to his master's satisfaction he could be sent to work in a mine where slaves did all of the work. The Romans operated coal mines in Britain, copper mines in Cyprus, and gold, silver, and lead mines in Spain. One silver mine in Cartagena, Spain, alone retained forty thousand slaves. Other slaves worked in quarries carving great slabs of marble used to build the glorious buildings of Rome.

Mines and quarries were the largest industrial sites of the ancient world, and to work in one of these was akin to a death sentence. Slave miners tunneled deep underground with primitive tools. The heat was intense, and cave-ins and explosions were common. In the book *Natural History*, first century Roman author Pliny the Elder describes gold mining by Roman slaves: "By the light of lamps long tunnels are cut into the mountains. . . . The miners carry the ore out on their shoulders, each man forming part of a human chain working in the dark, only those at the end seeing the daylight . . . men may not see daylight for months on end."[21] Historians estimate a slave who worked in such conditions survived, on average, only seven years.

While some philosophers such as Seneca preached that slaves should be treated like human beings, the Roman economy was so dependent on slavery that no one could imagine abolishing the institution. But as the centuries progressed, slaves acquired what were called permissions that somewhat eased their suffering. Around the second century, laws were passed that allowed slaves to keep wages they earned on their own. Laws also banned the torture, mutilation, and murder of slaves.

> **WORDS IN CONTEXT**
> *ergastulum*
> A slave lodging on a large estate.

City Slaves

In cities, slaves were bought and sold at large slave markets. These were filled with naked slaves who were paraded before the public with signs around their necks describing their strength or skills. Prices for slaves varied. Weak, small, or physically unattractive slaves were cheaper, while strong young boys and beautiful girls brought the highest prices.

Ordinary plebs might be able to afford one or two slaves, and these workers lived in close quarters with the rest of the family. City slaves worked as domestic servants—cooking, cleaning, caring for children, and serving food. Others worked as butlers, bodyguards, doormen, and gardeners. Patricians often owned several dozen household slaves along with thousands who labored on their country estates. Around AD 104 the Roman lawyer and author Pliny the Younger (son of Pliny the Elder) boasted in a letter to Emperor Trajan that he owned 4,116 slaves.

While masters were responsible for properly clothing and feeding slaves, some slaves starved and dressed in rags. Smaller homes lacked slave quarters, and slaves were forced to sleep in stairwells, hallways, or shacks outdoors. Like farm slaves, domestics could be whipped or beaten for slight infractions such as preparing food improperly or failing to clean up a mess. Sometimes the punishment was worse. The emperor Augustus described a dinner party where a slave broke an expensive glass. The master ordered the slave to be thrown into a pool of flesh-eating lamprey eels. Augustus intervened and saved the slave's life.

Even if slaves were not physically abused, their lives were degrading and abysmal. In his book *Deipnosophistae* or *Dinner-Table Philosophers*, third century author Athenaeus quotes a slave expressing his indignation:

> What can be worse than, while the guests are drinking,
> To hear the constant cry of, Here, boy, here!
> And this and that one may bear a chamber-pot
> To some vain beardless youth; and see around
> Half eaten savory cakes, and delicate birds,
> Whose very fragments are forbidden strictly
> To all the slaves—at least the women say so . . .
> And if he tastes a mouthful of solid food
> They call him a greedy glutton.[22]

In Their Own Words

Seneca on Slavery

Unlike most Romans, the intellectual Seneca believed slaves should be treated humanely at all times. In addition to writing numerous plays and essays, Seneca composed *Moral Epistles to Lucilius,* a series of 124 numbered letters about moral issues. It was published in AD 65, the year of Seneca's death. "Letter 47," excerpted below, explores issues between masters and slaves:

I laugh at those people who think it degrading for a man to eat with his slave. Why do they think it degrading? Only because the most arrogant of conventions has decreed that the master of the house be surrounded at his dinner by a crowd of slaves, who have to stand around while he eats more than he can hold, loading an already distended belly in his monstrous greed until it proves incapable any longer of performing the function of a belly, at which point he expends more effort in vomiting everything up than he did in forcing it down. And all this time the poor slaves are forbidden to move their lips to speak, let alone to eat. The slightest murmur is checked with a stick; not even accidental sounds like a cough, or a sneeze, or a hiccup are let off a beating. . . . It is just this high-handed treatment which is responsible for the frequently heard saying, "You've as many enemies as you've slaves." They are not our enemies when we acquire them; we make them so.

Quoted in John R. Welch, ed., *Other Voices: Readings in Spanish Philosophy.* Notre Dame, IN: University of Notre Dame Press, 2010, pp. 10–11.

The most fortunate slaves had talents that allowed them to work as bakers, barbers, tailors, artists, or musicians. In such cases, a master might help the slave establish a business or buy a shop. The master would then collect a percentage of the profits, while the slave was allowed to live as an independent person. If a business were successful, the slave could buy his freedom, earning the title freedman.

Slave work was not always manual labor, as Rodgers explains: "A Roman nobleman might have a Greek-speaking slave as his secretary or clerk, another as a librarian or tutor to his children and another as a bailiff or overseer of his land. These were often positions of importance and responsibility and sometimes of real, if limited, power."[23] Some slaves were not owned by individuals but by the state. These slaves worked as magistrates, accountants, and assistants in temples and government buildings throughout the empire.

Ports and Shopping Centers

With slaves working at about one-third of the jobs in Italy, free citizens struggled to earn a living. Wages were low in cities like Rome, and food and clothing were expensive. For example, a pound of chicken cost a tailor his entire day's wages. The price of a pair of boots was equal to a week's wages for a mule driver. In this environment even those with full-time jobs earned barely enough to support their families.

While life was a struggle, there was little unemployment in Rome mainly because of the Tiber River, which flowed through the heart of the city. The river allowed Roman ships to sail to the Mediterranean Sea, which was 27 miles (43 km) south of the city. The banks of the Tiber were lined with docks, warehouses, and offices where thousands of stevedores, sailors, porters, drivers, clerks, and agents began their labors at dawn.

Beyond the river, Rome supported numerous shops that sold food, wine, luxury goods, lumber, cloth, and spices from every corner of the empire. A survey conducted by the government in the fourth century mentions that Rome supported 254 bakeries and 2,300 oil shops, which pressed olives into oil for use in food, soap, perfume, medicine, lamps, and furniture polish. Some large specialty stores featured torches, candles, and tallow. Others sold only papyrus and parchment writing paper. One shop in the survey sold pepper, ginger, and other spices transported from the Middle East by Arab traders. Rome was also home to dozens of large specialty markets that sold cured meats, wine, cheese, wool, vegetables, fish, and edible delicacies.

Some shops were concentrated in huge plazas that acted as the shopping malls of the ancient world. In Ostia, the Pizazzale Delle Corporazioni, or the Square of Corporations, was a massive marble building 328 feet (100 m) long and 262 feet (80 m) wide. Ruins of the Pizazzale are still standing today, and visitors to the site can see row after row of small rooms that were once merchants' shops. The nature of each business was spelled out in mosaics, pictures and letters made from black-and-white clay tiles. Shops were rented by traders in flax and rope, furriers, leather merchants, marble traders, grain sellers, and importers of wild animals and elephant ivory. The merchants came from Egypt, Gaul, Sardinia, and port cities in North Africa such as Hippo Diarrytus, west of Carthage. The Pizazzale was also home to restaurants, taverns, and snack bars. One entire side of the plaza held a large theater where tired shoppers could relax with a play or musical performance.

Building Lasting Monuments

Beyond the shops and docks, the largest source of employment in Rome was in the construction trades. The Romans were expert builders who mobilized large numbers of workers to erect massive public buildings. These projects utilized experienced workers such as architects, engineers, draftsmen, master carpenters, stonemasons, painters, and decorators, along with thousands of unskilled workers.

The Colosseum, in the center of Rome, was the largest project ever built during the empire era, and its construction demonstrates the amazing abilities of Roman workers. The amphitheater, where gladiators battled to the death and prisoners were fed to the lions, seated fifty thousand spectators. It was oval in shape, 615 feet (187 m) long, 510 feet (155 m) wide, and 187 feet (57 m) high. The base area covered 6 acres (2.4 ha).

Construction of the Colosseum relied on building techniques that were highly innovative at the time. It was the largest building made from concrete, a Roman invention. Much of the concrete, made from a strong volcanic material called *pazzolana*, rubble, sand, and lime, remains intact today.

Stone carvers created pillars from travertine limestone that was quarried at a site 20 miles (32 km) distant and transported by wagons and mule drivers. The outer wall of the Colosseum was made from 3.5 million square feet (100,000 cubic meters) of hand-cut travertine stone. This was held in place by 300 tons (272 metric tons) of metal clamps made off-site by smelters and ironworkers. The building also required the skills of innumerable carpenters, brick and tile makers, marble workers, and plumbers who constructed the water and sewer systems.

The construction of the Roman Colosseum (pictured) provided work for thousands of skilled workers including architects, engineers, draftsmen, stone carvers, iron workers, carpenters, and plumbers as well as all manner of unskilled laborers.

Despite the complexity of the project, the Colosseum was built at an amazing speed. It was started around AD 70 and, with the work of approximately one hundred thousand laborers, was completed within a decade. As Rodgers notes, "By comparison, some cathedrals in medieval Europe took literally centuries to conceive, design and build."[24]

Equestrians

As a world center of commerce, Rome was home to banks, shipping companies, government contractors, and other large, profitable business. These enterprises were largely overseen by equestrians. As the name suggests, equestrians came from the Roman cavalry, which was originally made up of men with enough wealth to field a horse during times of war. Over the years there were far more men with horses than were necessary for war. By the first century AD, the equestrians acted as tax collectors, landlords, bankers, and government officials. Some held lucrative government contracts, such as those awarded to build roads and aqueducts.

> **WORDS IN CONTEXT**
>
> **pazzolana**
> Volcanic material used by Romans to make a type of long-lasting concrete.

While equestrians were necessary for the smooth functioning of the Roman empire, they were widely despised by average citizens. As classics professor Robert Knapp notes, Rome was an extremely unequal society where most plebs struggled to survive: "[The] social world was organized to oppress them. . . . Their sociopolitical situation was one of subjugation, whether it be to tax collector, state official, landlord, money-lender, or simply want; they were not free agents in any sense."[25]

The High-Ranking Senator

Equestrians were ranked on the social scale immediately below senators, officials who worked part-time writing laws to carry out the will of the emperor. Senators did not own businesses or work in commerce; they relied on the equestrian class to handle their business interests.

Most senators spent much of their considerable free time visiting their ancestral estates and overseeing their vast land holdings. As the

Looking Back

The Economic Role of Women

Although women made up about half the population in the Roman empire, they could not vote and did not normally attend school. However, Roman women worked extensively in the home and performed a variety of duties, as classics professor Robert Knapp explains:

The women do wool work, cook, make bread, light fires, draw water, make beds, and carry out some things around the house that require physical strength: grinding corn, kneading dough, cutting wood, getting wood, moving large containers around, and shaking out bedcovers. Women also help out in the fields and with harvesting when they are needed. [Jobs also] include grinding bread and selling in the market; keeping a shop; helping with agricultural work, especially during harvest; selling produce from the home, as well as delivering it to the market for sale; and being wet nurses.

Robert Knapp, *Invisible Romans.* Cambridge, MA: Harvard University Press, 2011, p. 80.

highest class of patricians, senators looked down on anyone, including equestrians, who worked for a living. In 44 BC Cicero summed up this attitude in an essay about suitable occupations for gentlemen:

First, those means of livelihood are rejected as undesirable which incur people's ill-will, as those of tax-gatherers and usurers. Unbecoming to a gentleman, too, and vulgar are the means of livelihood of all hired workmen whom we pay for mere manual labor, not for artistic skill. . . . Vulgar we must consider those also who buy from wholesale merchants to retail immediately; for they would get no profits without a great deal of downright lying. . . . Least respectable of all are those trades which cater for sensual pleasures: Fishmongers, butchers, cooks, and poulterers [chicken farmers]. . . . Add to these if you please, the perfumers, dancers.[26]

Despite such attitudes, Roman workers were extremely industrious. Their economic endeavors were central to a society that successfully supported millions of people for nearly five centuries.

Chapter Three

Life as a Legionnaire

With his flashing sword, brass breastplate, plumed helmet, and red cloak, the Roman legionnaire played a key role in the empire's military might. The legend of the Roman soldier began when Romulus and Remus founded Rome. The Latin word *legio* means "the chosen ones," and according to first century historian Plutarch: "The first thing Romulus did was to recruit all the able men for the armed forces. Each unit would have 3000 men on foot and 300 on horse, and he would give them the name legion because they were chosen from the bravest men around."[27]

For more than five hundred years, from the second century BC to the fall of the western Roman empire in AD 476, the legions defended and extended what was called *Imperium Romanum*, or the "power of the Romans." While the legions occasionally suffered minor losses at the furthest reaches of the empire, no greater army was assembled in Europe until the early 1700s when Prussian king Frederick William I turned his nation's military into the best fighting force in Europe.

The Most Desirable Soldiers

By the first century AD the Roman legion comprised roughly 250,000 men organized into 25 legions, or divisions. In addition there were 250 auxiliary units made up of troops recruited from local districts. By the year 200 the legion had grown to its maximum size, about 450,000 men in 33 legions backed by 400 auxiliary units.

As the world's first fully paid, professional fighting force, the Roman legion had strict requirements for recruits. All soldiers had to be Roman citizens, which included all freeborn men in Italy. After 212, full citizenship was granted to freeborn men throughout the empire—significantly increasing the eligible pool of soldiers. However, only a few units accepted freedmen, and slaves were banned entirely.

Once a man signed up for the legion, he was required to serve twenty-five years. If he deserted he faced execution if captured. While the terms were harsh, the life of a legionnaire provided economic opportunities not available to average plebs. Although a soldier earned only the same daily wage as an average laborer, he earned it every day, year after year. This contrasted with civilian workers, who were often underemployed or unemployed for months at a time. And while legionnaires were required to pay for their own armor, weapons, and other equipment, records show that the average soldier was able to save about 25 percent of his annual pay.

As a legionnaire advanced in rank, his pay could be twice that of a common soldier's. Centurions, officers who commanded divisions of one hundred men, could earn fifteen times more than a recruit. In addition, any legionnaire who survived his twenty-five year stint received a bonus equal to fourteen years' pay.

Because of the long term of service required of soldiers, the Romans needed to recruit only about ten thousand new legionnaires annually, out of a pool of 9 million eligible men. Most recruits were between seventeen and twenty-four. They were required to be unmarried, and most came from small farms or lived in poverty on city streets. As Tacitus notes, "It is chiefly the needy and the homeless who adopt by their own choice a soldier's life."[28]

Recruiters subscribed to the belief that the most desirable foot soldiers had few skills but required two specific qualities: *simplicitas*, or simple-mindedness, and *imperitia*, or ignorance. However, the legion also sought out cooks, carpenters, hunters, and butchers whose skills were useful to the army. In addition, the Romans needed priests, along with legionnaires who specialized in tasks such as bridge building, surveying, engineering, veterinary medicine, and even fortune-telling. These men, known as *immunes*, were excused from regular duties because they were valued more for their intellect

> **WORDS IN CONTEXT**
>
> *immunes*
>
> Roman legionnaires who did not fight; they worked as engineers, doctors, bookkeepers, and priests.

When in full battle gear, a Roman legionnaire (pictured) carried a sword, shield, and spear. He also wore a heavy iron helmet with flaps that protected his neck, face, and ears.

than for their prowess as fighters. And, as the Romans were known to be compulsive record keepers, educated legionnaires were needed to account for money, men, and supplies. As military expert Flavius Vegetius explained in the year 390 in his book *On Military Matters*,

> The army seeks in all its recruits tall, robust, quick-spirited men. But since there are many administrative units in the legions that need literate soldiers, those who can write, count, and calculate are preferred. For the entire record-keeping of the legion, whether of obligations or military fatigues [chores] or finances, is noted down in the daily records with even greater care than the . . . records of various sorts kept in the civilian world.[29]

Strenuous Training

The average legionnaire had little time for intellectual pursuits or deep thinking. Army life was routine and consisted of arduous drills that were repeated twice a day. Around AD 70, the historian Josephus glowingly praised the Romans for their commitment to training: "For the Romans, the wielding of arms does not begin with the outbreak of war, nor do they sit idly in peacetime and move their hands only during times of need. Quite the opposite! As if born for the sole purpose of wielding arms, they never take a break from training. . . . Their practice sessions are no less strenuous than real battles."[30]

Legionnaires practiced in full battle gear with swords, rectangular bronze shields, and spears with menacing 8-inch iron tips (20 cm). The soldiers wore heavy iron helmets with long flaps to protect the neck, face, and ears. Some were decorated with bronze ornaments, and the helmets of centurions, which were not worn in combat, featured tall plumes made from dyed horsehair. Legionnaires wore leather footwear with iron-studded soles. They marched on long-distance maneuvers with weapons in hand, carrying heavy leather packs on their backs. Each soldier was required to lug a three-day food supply, an iron cooking pot, clothes, and tools such as saws, shovels, and axes. After observing legionnaires with their packs, which weighed roughly 66 pounds (30 kg), the historian Josephus wrote, "The infantryman differs little from a loaded pack mule."[31]

Even at rest, soldiers could not escape the mule comparison: Their sleeping quarters resembled rows of stalls in a barn. Long brick barracks contained ten or more small rooms, each one providing sleeping quarters for a "tent unit" of eight soldiers. The group of eighty to one hundred men in each barrack, commanded by a centurion, was called a century unit.

A typical Roman fort contained ten rows of barracks, a large house for the commander, several workshops where weapons were made and repaired, a central oven for baking bread, a granary, and a bathhouse with large communal pools and toilets with running water. The soldiers' basic diet consisted of fruit, vegetables, porridge, cheese, salt pork, and sour wine. There were no mess halls or central kitchens. Every unit prepared its own meals, and the men ate together in a large room attached to the sleeping quarters.

Treating Illness and Injury

The hospital was another important feature at every fort, and each legion had one or more doctors. Sickness was taken very seriously since an epidemic could destroy a legion as fast as a well-armed enemy. However, Roman knowledge of medicine was limited. Doctors performed a variety of cures, some that were helpful, others that were deadly. Diseases were treated with herbal medicines, magical potions, and prayers to various gods. Roman doctors also believed in bloodletting, draining blood from a patient in the mistaken belief that bad blood caused sickness.

Legion doctors also needed to treat those injured in battle, and even simple wounds could be deadly. A stab wound that pierced the abdomen or intestines was often fatal. Doctors stitched up such wounds,

In Their Own Words

Military Maxims by Vegetius

In 390 military expert Flavius Vegetius wrote the Roman legion manual *De Re Militari*, or *On Military Matters*. The book offers advice on subjects as diverse as fighting with slingshots and riding armored elephants into battle. What follows are excerpts of Vegetius's general maxims for the battlefield:

> The more your troops have been accustomed to camp duties on frontier stations and the more carefully they have been disciplined, the less danger they will be exposed to in the field.

> Men must be sufficiently tried [trained] before they are led against the enemy.

> It is much better to overcome the enemy by famine, surprise or terror than by general actions, for in the latter instance fortune has often a greater share than valor. . . .

> To debauch the enemy's soldiers and encourage them when sincere in surrendering themselves, is of especial service, for an adversary is more hurt by desertion than by slaughter. . . .

> Few men are born brave; many become so through care and force of discipline.

> An army is strengthened by labor and enervated by idleness.

> Troops are not to be led to battle unless confident of success. . . .

> An army unsupplied with grain and other necessary provisions will be vanquished without striking a blow. . . .

> When an enemy's spy lurks in the camp, order all your soldiers in the daytime to their tents, and he will instantly be apprehended.

> On finding the enemy has notice of your designs, you must immediately alter your plan of operations. . . .

Flavius Vegetius Renatus, "The Military Institutions of the Romans," Digital Attic, 2007. www.pvv.ntnu.no.

while severely damaged limbs were amputated with saws and knives. There were no anesthetics to ease the pain other than great quantities of wine. Broken bones were set and packed with concoctions such as the following recommended by Pliny the Elder: "For broken bones, a sovereign remedy is the ashes of the jaw-bone of a wild boar or swine: boiled bacon, too, tied round the broken bone, unites it with marvelous rapidity. For fractures of the ribs, goats' dung, applied in old wine, is extolled as the grand remedy, being possessed in a high degree of . . . healing properties."[32] Arrow wounds were the most common type of injury and among the most painful to treat. Arrows had barbed heads and could not be pulled out without ripping the flesh. In some cases the arrow was pushed all the way through the wound until it came out the other side. If that was not possible, doctors used a tool called a scoop of Diocles. This instrument had two spoon-shaped cups on a long handle. These were forced into the wound, closed around the arrowhead, and pulled out without injuring surrounding flesh. Such practices often resulted in infection that led to a slow death. Accordingly, doctors were widely distrusted. As the military historian Martial wrote about his physician: "Until recently, Diaulus was a doctor. Now he is an undertaker. He is still doing, as an undertaker, what he used to do as a doctor."[33]

Making Camps

With the Roman legions pushing north, south, east, and west of Rome, doctors had a great deal of practice removing arrows and treating other types of battle injuries. By AD 43 the Roman legions had extended the empire's borders into Britain. In the following decade they would conquer much of present-day Germany, Romania, Bulgaria, Hungary, Poland, and Ukraine. In addition, the legions held territory in Syria, Israel, and Africa.

The Roman army was able to accomplish so much because their command structure was highly organized. When the legion was on the march, a team of surveyors and engineering units rode ahead with work teams. If necessary, temporary bridges over rushing rivers were constructed from casks and planks or by lashing several boats together.

The daily construction of a proper camp, or *castrum*, was another legion practice that helped the Romans triumph over their enemies. Castra were built even after soldiers had marched all day and an enemy was nearby. To build a castrum workers leveled large pieces of ground capable of holding hundreds of troops. Building engineers supervised teams of diggers who cut up layers of grass and grass roots, or sod. The sod was layered and packed tight to make walls, called parapets, that were at least 5 feet (1.5 m) high. Vegetius explains the importance of constructing a secure castrum:

[It] is very imprudent and dangerous to encamp in a straggling manner without some sort of entrenchment. It is an easy matter to surprise troops while [they are] refreshing themselves or dispersed in the different occupations of the service. The darkness of night, the necessity of sleep and the dispersion of the horses at pasture afford opportunities of surprise. A good situation for a camp is not sufficient; we must choose the very best that can be found lest, having failed to occupy a more advantageous post, the enemy should get possession of it to our great detriment.[34]

More permanent forts were called *castra stativa*, or standing camps. For these camps soldiers dug deep perimeter trenches from 9 feet (2.7 m) to 17 feet (5.1 m) wide and shored up the sod walls with tree branches. The trenches could not easily be crossed by enemies. Within the perimeter, the legionnaires constructed barracks, a hospital, and other buildings.

Whatever their length of use, castra allowed legionnaires to rest and gather strength for battle. They also acted as supply depots for soldiers fighting in the field. The Roman use of advance camps gave them an advantage against their less rested, less well-supplied British and German foes.

Fighting Techniques

In ancient times soldiers most often faced off against one another in large battlefield formations. Roman soldiers, dressed in iron and leather body

Looking Back

The Centurion

The Roman centurion had responsibility for the performance, training, appearance, and conduct of soldiers. British history professor Nigel Rodgers describes the centurions:

> Centurions needed to be not only excellent soldiers but literate, for they had to read and write orders and could have political or diplomatic roles. . . . A centurion was distinguishable by his silvered armor, his greaves (shin armor, also worn by legionnaires) and his transverse-crested helmet. He wore his sword on his left and his dagger on the right, but still carried a shield. Centurions were responsible for maintaining Roman discipline, using their *vitis* (vine cane) often to ferocious effect on their men. One centurion was killed by angry legionnaires during the mutiny on the Danube in AD 14. He was known as *cedo alterum* (Get me another!) due to his habit of beating soldiers until his cane broke. Centurions often took bribes from their men, for granting leave or exempting them from fatigues [chores]. But they paid for their privileges in blood, suffering disproportionately high casualties in battle, as they were expected to stand their ground to the end.

Nigel Rodgers, *Roman Empire*. New York: Metro, 2008, pp. 150–51.

armor, gloves, and leggings, lined up twelve men abreast. Each soldier occupied a space 3 feet (1 m) wide. In this way, ten thousand infantrymen formed a rectangular column 36 feet (11 m) wide and 1,500 yards (1,372 m) long, a length equal to five football fields. This column was surrounded by horse-mounted cavalry troops who protected the boundaries around the formation. As this fearsome column marched forward to meet an enemy, soldiers might assume a defensive formation called the tortoise. In this position legionnaires held their shields over their heads to create a shell-like armor meant to protect them from projectiles fired from slingshots and catapults.

When the legionnaires attacked a large group of opponents, they often did so in a triangular wedge formation, with one man in the lead, two behind him, three behind them, four behind them, and so on. Often the opposition was forced to split in two as the wedge moved forward through their ranks. The wedge also served to push the enemy together into tight spaces where movements were restricted. This was detrimental to German and British soldiers; in tight spaces they had great difficulty wielding their long swords. The Romans, on the other hand, used short *gladius* swords, less than 3 feet (1 m) long, which could be used to stab enemies in the abdomen regardless of how much room they had.

Other battle formations had names like the saw, the orb, and the skirmish. All had the same purpose—to break enemy battle lines, restrict the movements of individual soldiers, and divide troops into small, easily defeated groups. Those who tried to retreat were allowed to escape to the edges of the battlefield, where they were killed by cavalrymen wielding crossbows.

Weapons

In cases where enemies were stationed within forts or walled cities, legionnaires employed their advanced artillery weapons, called siege machines. Each century unit possessed a weapon called a *ballista*. This wood-framed armament, reinforced with iron plates and nails, was a large, freestanding crossbow. Torsion cords around 6 feet (2 m) long could be pulled back, and the loaded weapon could shoot a rock the size of an orange about 600 feet (182 m). The ballistae grew in size over the years, and by the fourth century the machines were capable of launching rocks that weighed up to 65 pounds (30 kg).

Another popular weapon, the onager, took its name from the term used to define the powerful kick of a wild donkey. This weapon, which had a much greater range than the ballistae, was a catapult similar to those used in the Middle Ages. The machine was loaded with stones or clay balls filled with explosive chemicals that burst into flames upon impact. According to fourth century historian Ammianus Marcellinus, after a stone was loaded into the onager, "the master artilleryman strikes the pin with a hammer, and with a big blow, the stone is launched towards its target."[35] The onager could drive a 110-pound projectile (50 kg) around 1,300 feet (396 m).

Artillery weapons and battle formations were among the many tactics used by Roman generals. But warriors recognized that it was easier to demoralize the enemy than to meet him face-to-face on a field of battle. To this end, the Romans employed a scorched-earth tactic called *vastatio*, which translates as "devastation." When marching through enemy territory, legionnaires plundered homes and farms. Houses were burned, crops and livestock were consumed or destroyed, and civilians (including women and children) were killed or enslaved. This systematic destruction denied the enemy food and often resulted in surrender before any combat was necessary.

> **WORDS IN CONTEXT**
>
> *vastatio*
>
> A Roman legion military strategy that consisted of destroying homes and farms to demoralize an enemy.

Romanizing Enemies

The Roman legion was a superior fighting force that quickly conquered its enemies. After the battles were over, legionnaires were able to hold territory with only occasional resistance. By the first century large field armies were grouped throughout the Roman border territories, and major camps were located on the Rhine and Danube Rivers in Central Europe and in Britain, Spain, Egypt, and Syria. However, soldiers had little to do while stationed in these frontier regions. This created two problems. Troops that did not fight lost their strength and discipline, which might lead to mutiny. In addition, the legionnaires were a constant drain

A catapult-like device called an onager is readied for use during a Roman siege on an enemy city. Artillery weapons, battle formations, and other tactics distinguished the Roman legions as the foremost warriors of their day.

on the imperial treasury, requiring food, clothing, shelter, medical care, and salaries.

Instead of supporting idle soldiers, generals put legionnaires to work on massive construction projects. The troops stayed in top physical shape working on government buildings, dams, bridges, baths, and aqueducts. These new structures also helped the Romans win respect and admiration from people they conquered.

The emperor Augustus was the first to institute the policy of "Romanization," building urban areas that resembled miniature Romes. Unlike many previous conquerors, Augustus did not engage in mass slaughter of vanquished people, as he explained shortly before his death in 14 AD: "I often waged war, civil and foreign, on the earth and sea, in the whole wide world, and as victor I spared all the citizens who sought pardon. As for foreign nations, those which I was able to safely forgive, I preferred to preserve than to destroy."[36]

By preserving foreign nations the emperor ensured that enemies would become allies as their lives improved under Roman rule. In pursuit of Romanization, Augustus and several emperors who followed built cities that were governed by veteran legionnaires. The city of Cologne, in Germany, was a prime example of this strategy. The legion conquered the people who lived on the east bank of the Rhine in AD 38 and then moved them to the west bank of the river. The vanquished tribes shared the city with two Roman legions that were stationed there.

In the following decades the legions developed Cologne, which became the provincial capital. By AD 100, the city was laid out like Rome, with paved roads set in a gridiron pattern. The military constructed a hospital, a theater, several temples, an aqueduct, public baths, and a central market square. Cologne was connected to other towns in the region by a well-paved, wide road complete with bridges and canals designed by Roman military engineers and built by legionnaires.

The Roman legions also constructed a massive wall around Cologne. Standing more than 8 feet (2.5 m) wide, 26 feet (8 m) high, and 2.5 miles (4 km) long, the mere sight of the wall was enough to discourage enemy warriors. Cologne continued to grow, and by the third century it was home to over twenty-five thousand people, serving as one of the most important trade and production centers in the empire.

Hadrian's Wall

While Cologne's wall was impressive, the barrier was small when compared to the most ambitious project ever undertaken by the Roman legion. Hadrian's Wall, which was ordered by the emperor Hadrian in AD 122, stretched across the entire length of northern England near its border with Scotland. Constructed with square stones, the wall is 73 miles (117 km) long, averages 10 feet (3 m) in width, and is 16 feet (5 m) to 20 feet (6 m) high.

Hadrian's Wall was the most heavily fortified in the empire, and much of the structure remains standing today. It contained lookout towers every one-third of a mile (0.4 km) and forts spaced at 1-mile intervals (1.6 km). Like other Roman forts, each one featured a commandant's house, hospital, granary, workshop, and barracks. Forts also had centrally heated bathhouses, hot water, and saunas where legionnaires gathered when off duty. In addition, a trench 10 feet (3 m) deep and 20 feet (6 m) wide was dug on the northern side of the wall. Incredibly, the wall was built in only three years, between 122 and 125, by a workforce numbering about five thousand.

Hadrian's Wall proved to be a treasure trove to historians. The legionnaires stationed at a fort called Vindolanda left behind over one thousand thin wooden tablets, around the size of postcards, that describe army life in northern Britain. Some tablets contain provision lists that record purchases of salt, fish sauce, goat meat, pork, and Celtic beer. Others describe the hardships Romans faced far from Italy's warm, sunny climate. Soldiers begged

their superiors for clothes to keep them warm in winter, including *subuclae*, wool vests, and *aboliae*, thick heavy cloaks. Legionnaires also complained about the gloomy weather. A soldier named Tacitus lamented, "The British sky is obscured by constant rain and clouds."[37]

Over two hundred individuals were mentioned by name on various tablets, but the native Britons were barely mentioned by the Roman conquerors. The only note that has been found seems to mock the fighting tactics of the locals: "[T]he Britons are unprotected by armor. There are very many cavalry. The cavalry do not use swords nor do the wretched Britons mount in order to throw javelins."[38]

The Vindolanda tablets show that officers were allowed to have their wives and children at the fort. One tablet includes a birthday invitation from a general's wife, Claudia Severa, to her sister, Sulpicia Lepidina: "Greetings. On 11 September, sister, for the day of the celebration of my birthday, I give you a warm invitation to make sure that you come to us, to make the day more enjoyable for me by your arrival. . . . Give my

Hadrian's Wall, portions of which can still be seen today (pictured), was the most ambitious wall-building project ever undertaken by the Roman legion. Ordered by the emperor Hadrian in AD 122, it stretched across the entire length of the English-Scottish border.

greetings to your [husband] Cerialis. My [husband] Aelius and my little son send him their greetings. I shall expect you, sister. Farewell, sister, my dearest soul, as I hope to prosper, and hail."[39]

Both Builders and Destroyers

The legionnaires, once the most deadly fighting force on earth, were builders as well as destroyers. Hardworking, efficient, and technically advanced, these men laid the foundations for dozens of modern cities, including London and Paris.

For better or worse the legions stabbed and slashed their way through enemy territory. With their centuries-old culture, they brought the iron fist of *Imperium Romanum* down on the vanquished, while Romanizing their ancient ways.

Chapter Four

Leisure and Entertainment

The Roman empire was founded by Augustus, a man who was as famous for pursuing pleasure as he was for his political programs. According to Pliny the Younger, the emperor Augustus "spent time on gambling, debauchery and extravagance."[40] When not amusing himself with personal vices, Augustus staged spectacularly bloody battles. On several occasions he hosted games at the Colosseum, attended by fifty thousand spectators, where hundreds of gladiators fought to the death. In one of the most famous blood-soaked events, Augustus staged a "sea fight" in which three thousand sailors on thirty warships battled one another on an artificial lake created specifically for the occasion.

Augustus was the richest man in the ancient world, and he maintained his grasp on power by spreading his wealth among plebs and patricians alike. In addition to sponsoring gladiatorial games, he provided Roman citizens with free wheat for bread. This set a precedent for later emperors, who followed similar policies which were mocked by author and satirist Juvenal in the early second century. The poet maintained that the average Roman only had two interests in life; a full belly and watching games. According to Juvenal, emperors were able to hold sway over the masses by providing "bread and circuses."[41]

A Place for Relaxation and Pleasure

Augustus was the first to build luxurious public baths, called *thermae*, which made up another key element of Roman society. The Baths of Agrippa, completed in 19 BC, had huge, artificial pools of hot, warm, and cold water. Admission to the sumptuous baths was free and open to all regardless of race, gender, or social status.

In later years dozens of thermae were built throughout the empire. These were important features of a society that valued relaxation and pleasure, concepts expressed by the Latin word *otium*, or "free time." Beyond the literal meaning, otium represented the best life has to offer, later summed up by the Italian phrase *la dolce vita*, or the sweet life.

Thermae were the heart of the sweet life for average Romans. After working from the first light of day until noon, most plebs dedicated their afternoons to a light meal and a short nap. This was usually followed by a visit to the thermae. According to historian J.P. Toner, to the average Roman "bathing was regarded as being as vital as eating, drinking, sex, and laughter."[42]

Thermae were more than pools where citizens could wash away the grime of city life. Like modern fitness centers, thermae included saunas, steam rooms, and massage tables. An outdoor exercise and gaming facility at a thermae was called a *palaestra*. This was a place to engage in exercises such as lifting weights, fencing, or playing racquetball or handball. (Women, in general, did not exercise.)

> **WORDS IN CONTEXT**
> *thermae*
> Public baths in imperial Rome; they often included shops, gymnasiums, and other amenities.

The finest thermae contained shops, cafes, libraries, lecture halls, and even art museums. These accommodations all served a larger purpose: They provided a place for people to mingle, make friends, gossip, and discuss politics and business.

Surrounded by Luxury

Thermae were so central to the Roman national identity that legionnaires built them to Romanize conquered peoples. The Turkish city of Constantinople, now called Istanbul, featured 153 small Roman-built baths and 8 magnificent, ornately decorated thermae. The city of Antioch was the site of a dozen thermae, while the military center of Timgad in North Africa had 8 small thermae for a population of about five thousand. These

The Roman custom of relaxing and visiting with friends in public baths was carried to other parts of the empire. Pictured is the Roman baths complex in the town of Bath in England.

numbers could not compare to Rome where, by the fourth century, there were over 850 medium-sized thermae and 11 exceptionally large, luxurious bathing complexes. These facilities were a source of public pride, and it was common for people to boast about the number of thermae in their town. In the second century the poet Aelius Aristides said his hometown of Smyrna, on the Aegean Sea, "had so many baths that you would be at a loss to know where to bathe."[43]

The interior decorations in the large thermae were so extravagant that architecture historian Fikret Yegül calls them "people's palaces."[44] The buildings featured fine multicolored marble, stone columns, exquisite mosaics, statues, murals, bronze hardware, and natural light provided by skylights in domed ceilings. The wonders of a sumptuous thermae led the poet Statius to write in the first century, "Be done with Toil and Care, while I sing of the baths/Bejeweled with shining marble!"[45]

The emperor Trajan built one of the grandest thermae ever constructed in Rome, but it was typical of all large public bathing facilities. The Trajan Baths could hold an estimated three thousand people, and the outdoor garden was home to restaurants, a theater, and a park filled with fountains, ornate trees, and flowers. This large public space was crowded with entertainers including jugglers, conjurers, mimes, musicians, and gymnasts.

Large baths also attracted motley groups of drunks, thieves, and pickpockets. (Togas and sandals belonging to bathers were among the items most commonly stolen.) Pliny the Younger complained about the excessive drinking habits of some who "lift up huge vessels [of wine] as if to show off their strength, and pour down the whole contents, then raise it up again to take another swig."[46]

Warm, Hot, and Cold Pools

All thermae featured three types of rooms for bathing. The *tepidarium* held a pool of lukewarm water. This was the most elaborately decorated room at the thermae, featuring red walls and elaborate mosaics, paintings, and arches. The room known as the *caldarium* was a huge space, as big as a medieval church. The caldarium featured a hot pool that emitted a thick veil of steam. An equally large room, called a *frigidarium*, contained a huge pool of cold water.

Bathers commonly began their visit in the lukewarm pool, moved on to the hot pool, and finished the experience with a quick plunge into the cold waters of the frigidarium. The entire experience lasted several hours. Some thermae also featured a large, shallow outdoor pool known as a *natation*, a steam bath called a *sudatorium*, and a sauna-like room called the *laconicum*.

Baths were heated by what was called a hypocaust system. A giant wood-fired furnace heated water stored in aqueduct-fed cisterns, the largest of which could hold 2 million gallons (7.5 million L) of water. The hot water circulated through an underground system of concrete tunnels and flowed to various pools. Hot air produced by the furnace flowed through hollow spaces in floors and walls, keeping them a pleasant temperature at all times of the year.

Huge, billowing columns of wood smoke, produced by immense boilers in the thermae, polluted the air in most Roman cities. In addition, countless trees were cut down across the empire to feed the furnaces. This resulted in widespread deforestation in the ancient world. As Alberto Angela notes, the great public baths were "ecological monsters that burned trees non-stop, day after day, month after month, year after year—for centuries, almost without interruption."[47]

Circus Maximus

Thermae were among several entertainment options available to average plebs. Another was chariot racing, a bloody, dangerous sport that was extremely popular with Romans from very early times. Rome's premier chariot racing track, the Circus Maximus (Great Circle), dates back to the sixth century BC. It was destroyed by fire and rebuilt several times over the centuries.

In AD 103, Trajan transformed the Circus Maximus from a run-down racetrack into an imperial monument. He built a brick, concrete, and stone wall three-stories high to enclose the track and replaced the wood seating areas with marble. Emperors and senators sat in the lowest seats near the concourse, equestrians sat behind them, and plebs were farthest from the action. In Trajan's time, the circus was about 1,950 feet (594 m) long and 645 feet (197 m) wide, an area that could contain nearly seven football fields. The track could seat an estimated three hundred thousand racing fans, about one-quarter of Rome's population. A low 1,100-foot stone island (335 m) called a *spina*, or spine, ran down the center of the track. It was decorated with racing trophies, statues, fountains, ornate columns, and tall, narrow four-sided monuments called obelisks.

The Circus Maximus was the greatest of three racetracks built in the city of Rome and among nine located in Italy. Several dozen other Roman-built circuses were located throughout the empire. Spain had nine

Crowds gather at the Circus Maximus for a day of chariot racing and other entertainments. Races, held throughout the year, attracted a cross section of Roman society.

circuses; Tunisia had six; Turkey had five; Greece, France, Portugal, and Algeria each had four; and Egypt held three.

Maximized Bloodshed

Romans celebrated more than one hundred holidays a year, and chariot races were held on each one. Admission to the circuses was free, and the action attracted a cross section of society. Street-corner astrologers and fortune-tellers offered betting advice for race fans. Food and wine merchants hawked their wares. Prostitutes dressed in feathers and boas danced to the music of drummers and flute players. These factors combined to make chariot races the most popular events in the empire. As Cicero writes, chariot races were "that kind of spectacle to which every sort of people crowd in the greatest numbers, and in which the masses find the greatest delight."[48]

Chariot racing teams, called factions, trained, equipped, and entered charioteers in the races. The four main imperial teams were White

In Their Own Words

The Noise of a Roman Bath

While thermae provided a sense of luxury otherwise missing in the lives of average Romans, the facilities were quite noisy. Seneca, who lived above a thermae, describes some of the bothersome noises:

I have lodgings right over a bathing establishment. So picture to yourself the assortment of sounds, which are strong enough to make me hate my very powers of hearing! When your strenuous gentleman, for example, is exercising himself by flourishing leaden weights; when he is working hard, or else pretends to be working hard, I can hear him grunt; and whenever he releases his imprisoned breath, I can hear him panting in wheezy and high-pitched tones. Or perhaps I notice some lazy fellow, content with a cheap rubdown, and hear the crack of the pummeling hand on his shoulder. . . . Add to this the arresting of an occasional roysterer [drunken merrymaker] or pickpocket, the racket of the man who always likes to hear his own voice in the bathroom, or the enthusiast who plunges into the swimming-tank with unconscionable noise and splashing. Besides all those whose voices, if nothing else are good, imagine the hair-plucker with his penetrating, shrill voice,—for purposes of advertisement—continually giving it vent and never holding his tongue except when he is plucking the armpits and making his victim yell instead. Then the cake-seller with his varied cries, the sausageman, the confectioner, and all the vendors of food hawking their wares, each with his own distinctive intonation.

Quoted in Frances Ellis Sabin, *Classical Associations of Places in Italy*. Boston: Marshall Jones, 1921, pp. 313, 315.

Faction, Red Faction, Blue Faction, and Green Faction. Like modern professional sports teams, the factions were large, powerful, and wealthy organizations. Each owned sprawling networks of stables and breeding farms for their horses. They ran exclusive training centers for charioteers, who were usually slaves or freemen willing to risk their lives for glory.

Each race featured twelve charioteers, three from each faction. There were two main types of competition, one employed two-horse chariots called *bigae*. The races most popular with the public featured four-horse chariots known as *quadrigae*. Sometimes teams added odd races for the sake of novelty. Three-horse chariots might compete and, on special occasions, ten horses were hitched to a single chariot. Whatever the number of horses, each race was seven laps, about 5 miles (8 km) in length.

> **WORDS IN CONTEXT**
> *quadrigae*
> Popular with racing fans, a type of chariot pulled by four horses.

Chariot racing was dangerous for a number of reasons. Chariots were very lightweight and easily upended. Crashes, called *naufragia*, or "shipwrecks," were common at the sharp 180-degree turns at each end of the track. The severity of accidents was aggravated because drivers wrapped the leather reins around their bodies to better control the horses. Drivers who were thrown from broken or overturned chariots might be dragged to their death by stampeding horses. Charioteers who managed to free themselves from the reins risked being trampled or crushed by the horses.

For those who survived with injuries, medical treatment was primitive. Pliny the Elder suggested applying boar dung to race-related wounds. For severe internal injuries, he recommended drinking a concoction made from boar dung and vinegar.

Despite the dangers, every race had a winner who was crowned with a wreath of palm leaves. Monetary prizes ranged from 5,000 to 60,000 *sestertii*, depending on the race. (By comparison, a donkey cost around 520 sestertii, while an average carpenter might earn 60,000 sestertii annually.) The few racers who won consistently were the sports celebrities of the ancient world. One of Rome's most successful charioteers, Appuleius Diocles, raced for the Red Faction beginning in AD 122. His career spanned twenty-four years—and during that time he won 1,462 races. When he retired his lifetime earnings totaled 35 million sestertii, an amount Juvenal estimated to be one hundred times as much as a wealthy lawyer earned in a lifetime.

Avid Fans

Drunken rowdy fans were a common sight at chariot races. Devotees of each faction dressed in team colors and sat together in groups, sometimes of ten thousand or more. Supporters yelled out elaborate coordinated cheers and sang team songs, oftentimes with words insulting fans of opposing teams. Fights were common in the stands and, on occasion, full-scale riots spilled out onto city streets.

Most fans remained dedicated to a single team throughout their lives. The White and Red factions were the first teams, although little of their early history is known. The Greens and Blues emerged during the early years of empire, and the Green faction was particularly popular with the poor. According to German history professor Ludwig Friedländer, fans were so zealous that the "whole huge population, from the rulers of the world down to the [plebs] and the slaves, were divided into four . . . hostile camps."[49]

The Romans believed that black magic spells and curses could affect their daily lives, and this was put to practice at the circus. Fans sometimes wrote spells on thin wooden sheets called curse tablets. These were placed in the stables of rivals. The verses appealed to the gods, asking them to lend their supernatural powers to the curse. One tablet found in North Africa reads, "Demon, I demand and ask of you that from this day, hour, and moment forward that you will torture the horses of the Greens and Whites. Kill Them! Kill also the charioteers. . . . Cause them to crash and leave no breath in their bodies!"[50] Curse tablets became so prevalent that laws were passed making it illegal to use black magic against charioteers.

Gladiator Games

Regularly scheduled chariot races were part of everyday life in the Roman Empire. Rome's other famous blood sport, gladiator games, were

Looking Back

"Why Does He Die So Sullenly?"

German history and linguistics professor Ludwig Friedländer describes the brutal treatment heaped on gladiators, especially slaves and prisoners who were forced to fight against their will:

The fainthearted aroused the anger of the populace, who thought it an insult [that] a gladiator should not be willing to die. The cowards were driven in with whips and hot irons to fight. The inflamed spectators shouted: "Whip him on, kill him, burn him! Why does he fear the sword? Why is he giving the death strokes so unwillingly? Why does he die so sullenly?" . . . Very often, too, the victor had to fight an understudy immediately after. In the intervals the blood–drenched ground was shoveled up by boys and Moorish slaves sprinkled fresh sand. The victors brandish their palms [wreaths], and the fallen were taken by men garbed as Mercury, the god of the nether world; others, wearing the mask of the Etruscan daemon Charon, probed [the losers] with hot irons, to see if they were shamming death. Hearses stood ready in anticipation, and on them [the dead] were borne through the gate of the Goddess of Death into the mortuary. Any who still showed signs of life were killed.

Ludwig Friedländer, *Roman Life and Manners Under Early Empire*, vol. 2. New York: Barnes & Noble, 1965, p. 61.

held only around ten times a year, usually on holidays. What these games lacked in frequency they made up for in carnage.

Like chariot racing, gladiator battles were a major source of Roman entertainment for centuries. They took place in amphitheaters like the Colosseum in Rome and smaller venues across the empire. The battles to the death between two heavily armed men originated as funeral games meant to honor the warlike spirit of the deceased. One of the earliest recorded games, in 183 BC, saw sixty pairs of gladiators clubbing, slashing, and stabbing one another at the funeral of the ruler Publius Licinius. The tradition of funeral games continued into the imperial era.

Gladiators were most often recruited from ranks of slaves, criminals, or prisoners of war. When there were not enough people available from these groups, freemen volunteered to fight. All were motivated by the promise of money and fame that accrued to gladiators who managed to survive.

Ancient artwork and reliefs depict at least fourteen different classifications of gladiator, each defined by the type of armor and equipment he used. However, most gladiators fell into two broad categories. Some were slow-moving, heavily armed and armored. Others wore little or no body armor, carried light weapons, and depended on speed and agility to fight. Romans favored matches that pitted lightly armed types against heavily armored men.

> **WORDS IN CONTEXT**
>
> *secutor*
>
> A heavily armed gladiator who fought with a full helmet and a large, heavy sword.

Light Arms and Slow Movements

The most common lightly armed gladiator was known as a *retiarius*. He carried no shield and wore only a loincloth, a metal shoulder guard, and a left arm protector called a *manica* made from leather, cloth, or metal. The retiarius carried a short sword, a three-pronged spear called a trident, and a heavy fishing net with weights on the ends.

The retiarius most often fought the *secutor*, who wore a greave on his left leg, a manica on his right arm, and, covering his entire face and

Spectators fawn over a victorious gladiator while the bloodied corpse of the loser is dragged away. Most gladiators were former slaves or prisoners, but those who repeatedly won their contests had a chance for both money and fame.

head, a full helmet with tiny eye holes. The secutor carried a wide shield of wood or leather and a large heavy sword.

In battle the *retiarius* whirled around the slow-moving secutor. There were attempts to trip the enemy with the fishing net before skewering him with the trident. The secutor tried to engage in close combat, protecting himself with his shield while lunging at the enemy with his sword. However, the heavy helmet not only reduced the hearing and sight of the *secutor*, it also limited the fresh air supply. This meant the gladiator tired much faster than his lightly armed opponent.

Oftentimes two secutores would face off against one retiarius who stood on a wooden platform called a *pons,* which was about 5 feet (1.5 m) off the ground. In this type of battle, the retiarius was also armed with stones about the size of an apple, which he hurled at the exposed parts of the enemy.

No Rules, No Referees

A variety of other gladiators entertained the masses. Some were lightly armed but carried huge shields. Others wore complete body armor but carried only small weapons. The type of gladiator known as the *crupellarius* was like a human tank. Tacitus describes these fighters as clad "in a complete covering of steel . . . and though they were ill-adapted for inflicting wounds, they were impenetrable to them."[51] Opponents would attempt to knock down these armored behemoths, beat their armor in with clubs, and chop them up with battle-axes.

On the day of the games, gladiators marched into the arena in a parade formation, led by a band and the patron of the game. On at least one occasion the fighters raised their weapons and shouted, "We who are about to die salute you!"[52] The gladiators started out hurling insults at one another and began fighting at a signal given by an official. There were no rules, referees, or time limits, but not all battles ended in death. A wounded man could drop his weapon, fall to his knees, and ask for mercy. His fate was truly in the hands of the crowd—or at least in their thumbs. Although countless movies show the thumbs down sign as a signal to kill, historians believe this was not the case. Thumbs down signaled that the victor should drop his weapon and let the defeated gladiator live. Thumbs up was a vote for the victor to stab the loser in the throat.

Entertainments Both Brutal and Benign

The Roman sense of leisure and entertainment ranged from the benign and simple pleasures of the baths to the brutal intensity of chariot races and gladiator combat. These diverse activities, enjoyed by Romans of nearly all classes, reflected their society—a society in which daily life could be both savage and civilized.

Chapter Five

Worshipping the Gods and Spirits

Religion was a central part of daily life in the Roman Empire, but citizens did not practice religion to enrich their inner spiritual lives. Romans believed that the gods could protect or punish them according to divine whims. In the Roman manner of thinking, bad luck was caused by ignoring or offending the gods. Good results were insured by properly appeasing the deities through prayer, sacrifice, and ritual. Above all, Romans were convinced that their gods and goddesses allowed them to rule the earth. As Cicero writes, "We owe our worldwide victories to piety, religion, and the knowledge that everything is directed by the will of the gods."[53]

The Romans were polytheists; they believed in a vast number of gods. Minor deities were invisible spirits who oversaw the smallest details of daily life, while the major deities looked and behaved like humans. They could be petty, generous, jealous, vengeful, and lethal.

Major Deities

Most of the chief deities originated in Greece but were renamed by the Romans. The main Greek god Zeus was called Jupiter or Jove in Rome. Jupiter was the king of the gods and, like other major deities, ruled many aspects of the world, including the sky, lightning, and thunder. He was the protector of the Roman people and selected them to rule the world. Like other gods, Jupiter was not worshiped for spiritual enlightenment but for personal gain. As Cicero explains, "Jupiter is Best and Greatest not because he makes us just or sober or wise, but because he makes us healthy and right and prosperous."[54]

Jupiter's wife (and sister), Juno—or Hera, in Greece—was the queen of heaven and protector of women, marriage, and childbirth, among other things. Minerva, based on the Greek goddess Athena, was the goddess of poetry, medicine, wisdom, weaving, and magic. Along with Jupiter and Juno, Minerva was part of what was called the Capitoline Triad, three supreme deities held in the highest esteem.

Other major deities included Mars, based on the Greek god of war Ares, and Mercury, the god of trade and travel the Greeks called Hermes. The wine-loving Romans held many enthusiastic festivals for Bacchus, the Greek Dionysus, who was the god of wine and ecstasy. The Greek goddess of love, Aphrodite, became Venus in Rome, while the goddess of agriculture, Demeter, became the Roman Ceres. Only Apollo, the god of the sun, prophecy, music, intellectual pursuits, and healing, retained his name in imperial Rome.

Spirits Great and Small

The Romans believed that the world was influenced not only by the major deities, but also by the vast number of spirits who intervened in peoples' lives on a daily basis. However, the Romans understood that many of these innumerable gods were unknown to them. This was particularly true when the Roman legions conquered new territories thought to contain abundant unfamiliar deities. To prevent divine interference, Roman military priests conducted a ritual called *evocatio* before the legions invaded new lands. This was meant to lure foreign spirits away from their posts. Priests addressed local deities and implored them to join the Romans. The gods who did so were promised that new temples would be dedicated in their names.

> **WORDS IN CONTEXT**
>
> *evocatio*
>
> A Roman ritual to summon the gods, especially to address foreign deities before an invasion.

One of the most famous foreign deities adopted by the Romans was Isis, revered by the ancient Egyptians as the goddess of nature, fertility, and magic. Isis spawned numerous religious societies called cults in the Roman empire, where the goddess was worshipped for centuries as the queen of heaven. (Cult, or *cultus* in Latin, means "care" and

The Romans believed that Jupiter, who was king of the gods, was their protector and had selected them to rule the world. Jupiter (depicted in this detail from a painting) was believed to hold power over the health and prosperity of Rome's citizens.

defines rituals and behavior dedicated to caring for a specific deity.) The Roman emperor Caligula was particularly enthralled with Isis. During his reign, which lasted from AD 37 to 41, new temples were dedicated to the goddess, and Isis festivals were added to the Roman holiday calendar.

The Roman pantheon also contained thousands of minor spirits called *numina*, who were perceived by the mind but not the senses. Numina were guardian spirits who oversaw infinite aspects of life, including all professions, every city, parts of the human body, concepts such as luck and victory, and aspects of nature such as flowers, forests, lakes, and mountains. Because they were so many numina, people worshipped only those who were important to their lives. A fisherman might pray to Tiberinus, the god of the Tiber River, to ensure his nets were filled with a large daily catch. A farmer might light incense for Bubona, goddess of cattle, or Segetia, the spirit of ripening grain. Every single piece of property hosted its own singular gods. Martial wrote of "the kindly deities of my tiny farm."[55]

There were many numina for childbirth and fertility, including Bona Dea and Camenae. The heart and other internal organs were ruled by numen Carna, while death was the realm of Dea Tacita, the "Silent Goddess." There was even a spirit named Cloacina who presided over the sewer systems of Rome.

Omens and Sacrifice

Whether deities ruled the heart or the sewers, they were believed to reveal their intentions in a variety of forms. For example, the god Fortuna might send an owl to a Roman's house to warn him to expect bad luck in the future. Jupiter might make eagles appear if destructive thunderstorms were imminent.

Professional soothsayers called augers looked for omens in nature. These men predicted the future by interpreting patterns of thunder and

In Their Own Words

Appealing to Foreign Gods

The Romans were extremely careful not to offend the gods and goddess worshipped by their enemies. Whenever legionnaires invaded a city, they offered prayers to unknown local deities and asked them to join the Roman cause. An example of the ancient prayer, first used to appeal to the gods of Carthage in the second century BC, was provided by the Roman author Macrobius around AD 400:

Whether you are a god or a goddess of these people who defend this city of Carthage, and you Most High, take back your favor in defense of this city and these people whom I attack. I pray, I beseech, I ask your indulgence, that you withdraw and desert these people and this city of Carthage, and that you relinquish the temples and sacred precincts of this city, go away without them, and incite these people and their city into fear of oblivion. Come then to favor Rome by crossing over to me and my army, and with our city tried and accepted as the location for your sacred precincts and holy rites, be propitious to me and the people of Rome, and my soldiers. If you make this happen, with clear and recognizable signs, I vow to erect temples for you and to initiate games in your honor.

Macrobius, "Saturnalia," The Roman World, May 12, 2004. www.ancientworlds.net.

lightning, the movements of animals, or the directional flights of birds. Many Roman leaders were obsessed with omens and made major decisions based on auspices, meaning "signs from birds." Those who ignored the auspices of augers did so at their own peril. Tacitus provided an account concerning the emperor Vitellius, who was preparing his army for battle in AD 69 when "a cloud of ill-omened birds [vultures] flew over his head and its density obscured the daylight."[56] Vitellius, who had been emperor little more than eight months, was quickly defeated and killed, having failed to heed the omen and retreat.

In addition to animal movements, the Romans believed that animal entrails were manipulated by deities to reveal aspects of forthcoming events. This led the Romans to regularly sacrifice lambs, chickens, young steers, and other animals. During sacrificial rituals animals were slit open with a special sacred knife. The entrails, including the liver, stomach, and intestines, were allowed to spill onto the ground. The arrangement of the entrails, including size, color, shape, and markings, purportedly disclosed divine messages to soothsayers.

Peace with the Gods

The object of Roman worship was to gain the goodwill of the gods and keep them happy. In order to do so it was necessary to maintain what the Romans called *pax deorum*, or "peace with the gods." *Pax* was interpreted to mean a state of order, cooperation, harmony, and control, as opposed to chaos and confusion. In order to maintain pax deorum, humans had to show respect to the gods and acknowledge their power. This was demonstrated through the strict repetition of ancient rituals in which every word and action took on supreme importance. Classics professor Jo-Ann Shelton explains:

> Year after year, century after century, the same procedures were repeated, the same words spoken in the same order, accompanied by the same actions. Since these rituals had proved their efficacy [value], no deviation was allowed. If one single word was mispronounced, one small action left out, the divine forces might not

listen or might even be offended. The slightest error in a religious procedure meant that it had to be done again, right from the beginning.[57]

Temples and Altars

Rituals were conducted at the thousands of temples located throughout the empire. Imperial temples were grand buildings most often situated on hills with unobstructed views where augers could watch birds in flight. Most temples featured wide stairways leading to porches where tall marble columns held up domed roofs. At the center of a temple, a walled inner room called a *cella* housed a statue of the temple's deity. A smaller second room beneath the temple was used for the storage of religious objects such as candles, incense, and other offerings. Weapons, armor, royal jewels, and other valuables looted during war were also locked in storage rooms, deposited there to give thanks to the gods for victory.

> **WORDS IN CONTEXT**
> *pax deorum*
> A state of harmony the Romans hoped to achieve with their deities through sacrifice, ritual, and prayer.

Each temple had a caretaker who guarded the valuables and oversaw a staff of slaves who cleaned, repaired, and maintained the building and grounds. Many temples also employed gatekeepers, clerks, guides, and gardeners.

Few worshippers ever entered the temples. Nearly all religious rituals took place at altars located outside the buildings. Individuals visiting a temple might burn incense or leave a small offering on the altar. During important ceremonies blood from sacrificed animals was spilled over the altar before prayers were recited. Parts of sacrificed animals, such as the liver or heart, might be burned upon coals at the altar. As Roman scholar Anthony Everitt notes, "Altars swam in the detritus of death."[58]

Altars were not located only at temples. Travelers set up roadside altars to offer thanks for safe journeys. Small altars could be found at

Looking Back

The Cult of Cybele

The Roman cult dedicated to the Cybele was among the most controversial cults in the empire, as classics professor Jo-Ann Shelton explains:

> When Roman officials first welcomed Cybele, Magna Mater, to their city, they knew little about the cult activities. What they soon learned shocked them because rites in honor of this goddess were quite unlike the calm, orderly, and methodical ceremonies of the state religion. Initiates to the cult of Cybele seemed to act in a state of emotional frenzy; their music was shrill and raucous. And the priests of the cult, called *Galli*, were particularly offensive to the staid and sober Roman temperament. *Galli* were eunuchs who castrated themselves upon entering the service of the goddess. Nor was this self-mutilation a unique experience in the priest's life. Apparently the *Galli* slashed their arms and shed their own blood during the annual celebration of . . . death and resurrection. As soon as Roman officials realized the nature of the cult activities, they took immediate measures to keep the cult tightly restricted.

Jo-Ann Shelton, *As the Romans Did*. New York: Oxford University Press, 1998, p. 399.

rivers, hot springs, groves of trees, and other places in the natural world where divine powers were believed to be strong. Numerous altars could be found in most cities as well. In Rome the Ara Maxima, or Greatest Altar, was dedicated to Hercules, the demigod (half human, half divine) son of Jupiter renowned for his strength and adventures. The Ara Maxima attracted businessmen who struck deals there before making sacrifices to ensure success.

Worship at Home

Every home had at least one altar, and most Romans conducted personal religious ceremonies on a daily basis—focused mainly on concerns such as health, work, and money. The paterfamilias acted as the family priest and led worship for the entire family. The head of the household was also responsible for maintaining the family shrine, called a *laraium*. This shrine honored domestic guardian deities called *lares*, who protected and influenced events within the home.

The laraium usually was located in the garden, atrium, or bedroom of the home. It might be a small freestanding shrine or just a corner of a room where a lares statue or painting was positioned. Every morning the paterfamilias lit incense at the laraium. Before dinner the entire family gathered at the laraium to make an offering that might include meat, fruit, flowers, wheat, wine, milk, or honey.

> **WORDS IN CONTEXT**
> *laraium*
> A family shrine kept in the home used to honor domestic deities called lares.

One of the most important jobs of the paterfamilias was maintaining a proper relationship with the dead, and this was also done at the laraium. Romans believed that wandering malevolent spirits of the dead, called *lemures,* could steal away healthy family members and take them to the underworld. To prevent this, the Romans held the festival of Lemuria on May 9, 11, and 13 to exorcise their homes of the lemures. On each night of the holiday, after the family had gone to sleep, the paterfamilias washed his hands three times and walked through the home barefoot. He sprinkled spring water throughout the house and threw nine black beans over his shoulder. The beans were thought to contain a life force that would appease the dead. When this ritual was complete, the head of the household felt assured that the dead would leave his family alone.

Blood Cults

The ancient Romans often participated in cults, also known as mystery religions. Cult practices involved secret rites and doctrines known only to initiates. Many of the cults were based on deities of the east such as Isis. One of the most popular was called Mithraism, which was open only to men.

Mithras was originally a Persian god who was adopted first by the Greeks, then by the Romans. It was believed that Mithras fought and killed a wild bull in a cave at the beginning of time. The spilled blood of the bull was responsible for creating all life on Earth. Because of its focus on violent bullfighting, Mithraism was particularly popular among legionnaires. During secret rites they gathered in cave-like underground rooms called *mithraeum*.

Hundreds of mithraeum, all featuring standardized decorations, have been unearthed by archeologists. The rooms are long tunnels lined with benches. The wall at the end of the tunnel features a painting or statue of Mithras with mysterious symbolic imagery. The artworks depict Mithras straddling a fallen bull and cutting its throat with a large knife held in his right hand. Wheat sprouts from the bull's tail, a dog drinks the bull's blood, and a serpent, crow, and scorpion are shown, along with the sun and moon. No written explanations of these images have survived. Archeologists speculate they show Mithras sharing a meal of bull parts with the sun, while the creatures represent various gods.

One of the bloodiest Roman cults was dedicated to the Turkish goddess Cybele. The goddess was called the great mother of all things, and her cult was open to both men and women. Those who were initiated into the cult were made to lie down in a trench. They were covered with boards drilled with holes. A bull was led over the trench and sacrificed. In what might have been a purification or cleansing ritual, the belly of the bull was slit open and gallons of blood flowed down on the initiate below. Another ritual was based on the belief that Cybele's lover Atys had been unfaithful to her. Atys was so ashamed that he castrated himself. The most fanatical followers in the cult showed their loyalty to Cybele by castrating themselves with dull implements such as pieces of flint.

Vestal Virgins

One of the most important Roman cults, the vestal virgins, was dedicated to Vesta, the goddess of hearth and home. The order was open only to women priests, six vestal virgins who were chosen for the cult when they were between the ages of six and ten. In the second century the author Aulus Gellius described the requirements a girl must meet to qualify as a vestal virgin: "Both her father and mother must be alive. She must not be

One of the most important Roman cults was dedicated to Vesta, the goddess of hearth and home. The order's vestal virgins (some of which are depicted around an altar) were trained from a young age to perform religious duties in service of the goddess.

handicapped by a speech or hearing problem or disfigured by some physical defect. . . . Neither one nor both of her parents may have been slaves or may engage in demeaning occupations."[59] The chosen girls were taken to live in the House of Vesta, adjacent to the round Temple of Vesta in Rome. The priests served for thirty years, vowing to remain celibate during that entire time. Those who violated their vows faced the prospect of trial and execution.

During the first ten years of service vestal virgins were trained to perform religious duties in service of the goddess; the second ten years they carried out those duties; and the last ten years were spent training novices. The most important duties of the vestal virgins concerned fueling the everlasting fire that burned night and day under the altar of Vesta. It was believed that if the fire went out, Rome would face destruction. In addition to maintaining the eternal flame, vestal virgins cleaned and purified the shrine with spring water each morning and assisted with public holy rites.

After thirty years of service the vestal virgins were free to return to their families and marry if they wished. However, few left the temple. According to first century BC Greek historian Dionysius of Halicarnassus, those who did choose to leave lived "lives which are neither enviable nor very happy. And therefore, taking the unhappy fates of these few as a warning, the rest of the virgins remain in service to the goddess until their deaths; at which time another virgin is appointed . . . to take the place of the deceased."[60]

Festivals and Holidays

March 1, the start of the Roman New Year, was the most important holiday at the Temple of Vesta. It was the only day of the year when the inner sanctum of the temple was open to all women. They entered barefoot and brought gifts and offerings for Vesta. The culmination of the holiday was the ceremony in which the eternal fire was allowed to burn very low before being symbolically relit with two sticks rubbed together.

New Year was among dozens of religious holidays celebrated by the Romans. The most popular was the winter solstice celebration of Saturnalia, which lasted from December 17 to 23. Saturnalia was a time of joy, goodwill, and gift giving. Stores and businesses closed their doors so workers could celebrate.

In Rome Saturnalia began with a religious ceremony at the Temple of Saturn. Afterward, the emperor and other patricians provided a huge public feast, free to all. Other days of the holiday were filled with drinking, family dinners, and visits with neighbors and friends. Even slaves were allowed to enjoy Saturnalia. They were given gifts and were exempt from punishment. For one day of the holiday social roles were reversed, and slaves were allowed to treat their masters with lighthearted disrespect. In addition, slaves might be served a banquet by their masters, although they had to prepare it and clean up afterward.

Persecution of Jews and Christians

With their polytheistic beliefs, Romans were tolerant of most religions. Judaism and Christianity were two exceptions. Both religions were monotheistic, which meant worshippers believed in a single god. Christians were particularly critical of polytheism.

Jews, who lived in all parts of the Roman empire, were often targets of official persecution. Emperor Tiberius forced Jews to burn their vestments and other religious objects. Around AD 121 the historian Suetonius wrote that Tiberius tried to rid Rome of Jews: "He distributed Jewish youths, under the pretense of military service, among the provinces noted for an unhealthy climate; and dismissed from the city all the rest of [the Jews] as well as those who were proselytes to that religion, under pain of slavery for life, unless they complied."[61]

Early Christians, most of whom were originally Jewish, were also persecuted because Roman officials believed Christianity was a dangerous cult. By the early second century, Christians could be charged with treason for their refusal to acknowledge the Roman gods and worship at the temples. After the emperor Marcus Aurelius came to power in the 160s, Christians were regularly tortured and executed. In 177 the historian Eusebius described the persecution of Christians by a mob in Lyon, France (once part of the Roman Empire): "They endured nobly the injuries heaped upon

Roman soldiers discover Christians worshipping secretly. The Romans saw Jews and Christians as disruptive forces. Both were persecuted; many were enslaved or tortured and executed.

them by the populace; clamors and blows and draggings and robberies and stonings and imprisonments, and all things which an infuriated mob delight in inflicting on enemies and adversaries."[62]

The persecution ended around 310 when the emperor Constantine became the first Roman ruler to convert to Christianity. While Constantine tolerated all beliefs, in 395 the emperor Theodosius I made Christianity the official state religion of the Roman empire.

An Enduring Civilization

When Christians achieved state power, they banned many Roman religious holidays. However, Saturnalia was too popular to terminate, so Christians transformed the festival. According to Shelton, "Its place was conveniently taken in the Christian calendar by Christmas, but many of the festivals which surrounded the celebration of Saturn were absorbed into the celebration of Christ's birth. The Christians wisely absorbed what they could not eradicate."[63]

Even after Christian emperors took control of the Roman Empire, millions continued to worship Saturn, Bacchus, Venus, and other ancient deities, keeping the religious beliefs of everyday Roman citizens alive. Whatever gods the Romans believed in, their empire faced serious problems that prayers alone could not solve. By the fourth century the empire was shaken by poor harvests, starvation, a faltering economy, civil strife, and fast-spreading diseases such as the plague and malaria. At the same time, Rome's enemies in Germany, Persia, and elsewhere were growing in strength even as the empire's power weakened. The Roman Empire declined and finally collapsed in 476. While the political authority of the emperors was over, the culture of the Roman people continued to influence western civilization for centuries that followed.

Source Notes

Introduction: A Vibrant Society

1. Alberto Angela, *A Day in the Life of Ancient Rome*. New York: Europa, 2010, p. 19.

2. Angela, *A Day in the Life of Ancient Rome*, p. 21.

Chapter One: Home and Family

3. Seneca, "Seneca's *Essays* Volume 1," The Stoic Legacy to the Renaissance, March 11, 2004. www.stoics.com.

4. Quoted in Jo-Ann Shelton, *As the Romans Did*. New York: Oxford University Press, 1988, p. 24.

5. Quoted in *Herald Sun*, "My Castle, My Self," September 26, 2010. www.heraldsun.com.

6. Juvenal, "Satire 3," trans. G.G. Ramsey, Tertullian Project, 2008. www.tertullian.org.

7. Juvenal, "Satire 3."

8. Quoted in Ludwig Friedländer, *Roman Life and Manners Under Early Empire*, vol. 1. New York: Barnes & Noble, 1965, p. 21.

9. Quoted in Nigel Rodgers, *Roman Empire*. New York: Metro, 2008, p. 336.

10. Angela, *A Day in the Life of Ancient Rome*, p. 17.

11. Petronius, *Satyricon Of Petronius Arbiter*, trans. W.C. Firebaugh. Whitefish, MT: Kessinger, 2004, p. 51.

12. Quoted in Lori A. Smolin and Mary B. Grosvenor, *Nutrition And Eating Disorders*. New York: Infobase, 2005, p. 95.

13. Quoted in Neil W. Bernstein, "Aulus Gellius 6.12," Diotima, Stoa Consortium, 2001. www.stoa.org.

14. Ovid, "The Art of Beauty," Internet Sacred Text Archive, 2012. www.sacred-texts.com.

15. Quoted in Shelton, *As the Romans Did*, p. 306.

Chapter Two: Working for a Living

16. Horace, "The Book of the Epodes," Authorama, 2012. www.authorama.com.

17. Quoted in Robert Knapp, *Invisible Romans*. Cambridge: Harvard University Press, 2011, p. 130.

18. Rodgers, *Roman Empire*, p. 465.

19. Quoted in Walt Stevenson, "Selection of Roman Slave Laws," University of Richmond, August 1, 2012. https://facultystaff.richmond.edu.

20. Quoted in Gregory S. Aldrete, *Daily Life in the Roman City: Rome, Pompeii and Ostia*. Westport, CT: Greenwood, 2004, p. 67.

21. Quoted in John Simkin, "Slavery in the Roman Empire," Spartacus Educational, 2012. www.spartacus.schoolnet.co.uk.

22. Athenaeus, "The Deipnosophists," trans. C.D. Yonge, Attalus, September 12, 2011. www.attalus.org.

23. Rodgers, *Roman Empire*, p. 474.

24. Rodgers, *Roman Empire*, p. 288.

25. Knapp, *Invisible Romans*, p. 104.

26. Marcus Tullius Cicero, *De Officiis*, trans. Walter Miller. Cambridge: Harvard University Press, 1913, p. 150.

Chapter Three: Life as a Legionnaire

27. Quoted in José Sánchez Toledo, *Imperium Legionis*. Madrid: Andrea, 2004, p. 8.

28. Cornelius Tacitus, *Annals of Tacitus*, trans. Alfred John Church and William Jackson Clark. New York: Macmillan, 1906, p. 115.

29. Quoted in Knapp, *Invisible Romans*, p. 204.

30. Quoted in Shannon E. French, *The Code of the Warrior: Exploring Warrior Values Past and Present*. Lanham, MD: Rowman & Littlefield, p. 76.

31. Quoted in Shelton, *As the Romans Did*, p. 261.

32. Pliny the Elder, "The Natural History of Pliny," Internet Archive, 2012. http://archive.org.

33. Martial, "Epigrams I," ed. E. Capps, Internet Archive, 2012. http://archive.org.

34. Flavius Vegetius Renatus, "The Military Institutions of the Romans," Digital Attic, 2007. www.pvv.ntnu.no.

35. Quoted in William Gurstelle, *The Art of the Catapult*. Chicago: Chicago Review, 2004, p. 128.

36. Augustus, "The Deeds of the Divine Augustus," trans. Thomas Bushnell, Internet Classics Archive, 2009. http://classics.mit.edu.

37. Quoted in Harry Mount, "Hadrian's Soldiers Writing Home," *Telegraph*, July 21, 2008. www.telegraph.co.uk.

38. Quoted in Centre for the Study of Ancient Documents, "Vindolanda Tablets Online," Oxford, 2012. http://vindolanda.csad.ox.ac.uk.

39. Quoted in Centre for the Study of Ancient Documents, "Vindolanda Tablets Online."

Chapter Four: Leisure and Entertainment

40. Quoted in Ray Laurence, *Roman Passions: A History of Pleasure in Imperial Rome*. London: Continuum, 2009, p. 21.

41. Quoted in Eckart Köhne and Cornelia Ewigleben, eds., *Gladiators and Caesars: The Power of Spectacle in Ancient Rome*. Berkeley: University of California Press, p. 8.

42. J.P. Toner, *Leisure and Ancient Rome*. Cambridge, UK: Polity, 1995, p. 53.

43. Quoted in Fikret Yegül, *Bathing in the Roman World*. New York: Cambridge University Press, 2010, p. 3.

44. Yegül, *Bathing in the Roman World*, p. 8.

45. Quoted in A.S. Kline, "Publius Papinius Statius," Poetry in Translation, March 2, 2012. www.poetryintranslation.com.

46. Quoted in Yegül, *Bathing in the Roman World*, p. 26.

47. Angela, *A Day in the Life of Ancient Rome*, p. 273.

48. Quoted in Toner, *Leisure and Ancient Rome*, p. 35.

49. Friedländer, *Roman Life and Manners Under Early Empire*, vol. 2, p. 28.

50. Quoted in Robert K. Sherk, *The Roman Empire from Augustus to Hadrian*. Cambridge: Cambridge University Press, 1994, p. 217.

51. Quoted in Konstantin Nossov, *Gladiator: Rome's Bloody Spectacle*. New York: Osprey, 2009, p. 71.

52. Quoted in Gary Edward Forsythe, "Gladiator," International World History Project, 2006. http://history-world.org.

Chapter Five: Worshipping the Gods and Spirits

53. Quoted in Friedländer, *Roman Life and Manners Under Early Empire*, vol. 3, p. 85.

54. Quoted in Shelton, *As the Romans Did*, p. 371.

55. Quoted in Shelton, *As the Romans Did*, p. 369.

56. Tacitus, *The Histories,* trans. W. Hamilton Fyfe, Project Gutenberg, October 27, 2012. www.gutenberg.org.

57. Shelton, *As the Romans Did*, p. 370.

58. Anthony Everitt, *Augustus*. New York: Random House, 2006, p. 30.

59. Quoted in Robert B. Kebric, *Roman People*. Mountain View, CA: Mayfield, 1993, p. 208.

60. Quoted in Shelton, *As the Romans Did*, p. 386.

61. C. Suetonius Tranquillus, "The Lives of the Twelve Caesars," trans. Alexander Thomson, Project Gutenberg, October 22, 2006. www .gutenberg.org.

62. Eusebius, in "Church History (Book VI)," translated by Arthur Cushman McGiffert. From *Nicene and Post-Nicene Fathers,* Second Series, vol. 1. Edited by Philip Schaff and Henry Wace (Buffalo, NY: Christian Literature, 1890). Revised and edited for New Advent by Kevin Knight, 2009. New Advent, 2009. www.newadvent.org.

63. Shelton, *As the Romans Did*, p. 383.

For Further Research

Books

Tony Allen, *Exploring the Life, Myth, and Art of Ancient Rome*. New York: Rosen, 2011.

Caroline H. Harding and Samuel B. Harding, *The City of the Seven Hills: A Book of Stories from the History of Ancient Rome*. Bayside, NY: A.J. Cornell, 2011.

Hal Marcovitz, *Ancient Rome*. San Diego, CA: ReferencePoint, 2012.

Timothy J. Moore, *Roman Theatre*. Cambridge, UK: Cambridge University Press, 2012.

Don Nardo, *Ancient Roman Art and Architecture*. Farmington, MI: Lucent, 2012.

Don Nardo, *Roman Mythology*. Farmington, MI: Lucent, 2012.

Websites

A History of Ancient Rome (www.historylearningsite.co.uk/a_history _of_ancient_rome.htm). This site features brief descriptions and pictures of many aspects of ancient Roman life, including housing, medicine, baths, government, and education.

Illustrated History of the Roman Empire (www.roman-empire.net). This comprehensive site has interactive pages about Roman history, emperors, religion, society, and the legion. Ancient maps and models recreate vistas of fourth century Rome, while amazing photographs of ruins prove the durability of Roman construction techniques.

Internet Ancient History Sourcebook: Rome (www.fordham.edu/ halsall/ancient/asbook09.asp#The Empire and Provinces). The Romans were excellent scholars and their historians, geographers, philosophers, and other professionals wrote scores of works that describe cities, provinces, military campaigns, and many aspects of daily life as it was lived two thousand years ago. This site contains texts written by Augustus, Juvenal, Pliny the Elder, and dozens of others.

The Military Institutions of the Romans (www.pvv.ntnu.no/~madsb /home/war/vegetius). This site features an English translation of the Roman military manual *De Re Militari*, or *On Roman Military Matters*, written in AD 390 by legion expert Flavius Vegetius. This fascinating book covers a wide range of subjects from teaching recruits to use slingshots to riding armored elephants into battle.

Rome Reborn (www.romereborn.virginia.edu). Rome Reborn features 3D digital models that illustrate the urban development of ancient Rome from the first settlement around 1000 BC to the early Middle Ages around AD 550. Most of the work featured is based on the look of Rome in the late empire era, circa 320, when the city had reached the peak of its population.

Vindolanda Tablets Online (http://vindolanda.csad.ox.ac.uk). Hosted by Oxford University, this website features photos and translations from hundreds of tablets written by Roman legionnaires stationed along Hadrian's Wall in the second century AD. The legionnaires described their food, clothing, religious ceremonies, celebrations, and military tactics.

Index

Note: Boldface page numbers indicate illustrations.

altars, 75–76
Angela, Alberto, 19, 23, 60
Antioch, 57
Apollo (deity), 70
aqueducts, 8, 37, 51, 52, 59
Ara Maxima (Greatest Altar),
 76–77
Aristides, Aelius, 58
Augustine (theologian), 27
Augustus (emperor), 8, 13, 56
 Romanization policy of, 51–52

ballista (weapon), 49
Baths of Agrippa, 56–57
battle formations, 47–49
bigae (two-horse chariots), 63
black magic, 64
blood cults, 78
Bona Dea (numen), 72
Britons, 53
Bubona (deity), 72
building techniques, 36

Caligula (emperor), 72
Camenae (numina), 72

Capitoline Triad, 70
Carna (numen), 72
castra (military encampments), 47
Cato the Elder, 13
Catullus, 16
centurions, 41, 48
century unit, 44
Ceres (deity), 70
chariot racing, 60, 61, 63–64
 fans at, 64
Christianity, 82–83
Christians, persecution of, 81–82,
 82
Cicero (Roman senator), 13,
 38–39, 69
 on chariot races, 61
 on Jupiter, 70
circuses (race tracks), 60–61
Circus Maximus, 17, 60–61, **61**
cities, 9
citizenship, 40
class structure, 9–11
Cloacina (numen), 72
clothing
 men's, 21–22
 soldiers', 53
 women's, 24–25
Cologne, Germany, 52

Colosseum, 35–37, **36,** 56

Columella (Roman scholar), 29

commerce, 34–35

Constantine (emperor), 82

Constantinople, 57

convivia (banquets), **20,** 21

Corrina (Ovid's mistress), 25

cosmetics, 25

crupellarius (armored gladiator),
  68

cults, 71–72
  blood, 78
  of Cybele, 76

Cybele, cult of, 76, 78

Dea Tacita (numen), 72

deities
  foreign, appeals to, 73
  major, of Roman religion, 69–70

dining, 19–21

dining rooms (*triclinium*), 19

Diocles, Appuleius, 63–64

Dionysius of Halicarnassus, 80

Dionysus (deity), 70

domus/domūs (house/houses), 16,
  18–19

dwellings
  of patricians, 16
  of plebians, 13–16

enemies
  appeals to deities of, 73
  Romanization of conquered,
    51–52

entertainment/leisure activities,
  56
  chariot racing, 60–61, 63–64
  gladiator games, 64–68
  public baths, 56–60, 62

equestrians, 22, 37

ergastulum (slave lodging), 31

Everitt, Anthony, 75

evocatio (ritual), 70

families/family life, 12–13
  home worship in, 77

farm labor, 28–30

festivals, 80–81

fighting techniques, 47–49

Fortuna (deity), 72

foundlings, 27

Frederick William I (Prussian
  king), 40

Friedländer, Ludwig, 64, 65

Gellius, Aulus, 79–80

gladiatorial games, 64, **67,** 68

gladiators
  brutal treatment of, 65
  types of, 66–67

gods. *See* deities

Great Fire of Rome (AD 64), 16,
  17

Hadrian's Wall, 52–53, **54**

Hercules (demigod), 76–77

holidays, 61, 80–81

Horace (poet), 26

immunes, 41, 43
Imperium Romanum, 40
insulae (apartment buildings),
    13–15, **14,** 23
    burning/collapsing of, 15–16
Isis (deity), 71
    cult of, 78

Jews, persecution of, 81
Josephus (historian), 44
Jupiter (deity), 69–70, **71,** 72
Juvenal (poet), 15, 16, 56

Knapp, Robert, 37, 38

laraium (family shrine), 77
latrines, public, 15
legionnaires, 9, 40–41, **42**
    as both builders/destroyers, 55
    in Britain, 53
    training of, 43–44
leisure activities. *See*
    entertainment/leisure activities
lemures (spirits of the dead), 77
Lemuria, festival of, 77
life expectancy, 13

Macrobius (writer), 73
Marcellinus, Ammianus, 50
marriage, 13
Martial (poet), 46, 72
medicine, 44, 46, 63
Minerva (deity), 70
mines/mining, 31

mithraea, 78
Mithraism, 78
Mithras, 78
Moral Epistles to Lucilius (Seneca),
    33

Natural History (Pliny the Elder),
    31
numina (minor deities), 72

onager (catapult), 50, **51**
On Military Matters (Vegetius),
    43, 45
otium (free time), 57, 59
Ovid (poet), 25

palaestra (exercise facility), 57
paterfamilias, 12, 13, 77
patricians, 9
    dwellings of, 16, 18–19
pax deorum (peace of the gods),
    74, 75
pazzolana (construction material),
    36, 37
Petronius (writer), 20
Piazzale delle Corporazioni
    (Ostia), 35
plebeians/plebs, 9–10, 11
    diets of, 15
    dwellings of, 13–15, **14**
Pliny the Elder, 31, 46, 63
polytheist, 69
ports, 34
public baths (*thermae*)**,** 52, 56–60

in England, **58**
heating of, 59–60
noises of, 62
rooms in, 59

quadrigae (four-horse chariots),
    63
religion, Roman, 69
    altars/temples, 75–77
    Christianity, Roman conversion
        to, 82–83
    major deities of, 69–70
    pax deorum and, 74–75
    personal ceremonies of, 77
    spirits and, 70–72
    See also cults
retiarius (gladiator), 66–67
Rodgers, Nigel, 28, 34, 48
Roman Empire
    Christianity becomes official
        religion of, 82–83
    class structure of, 9–11
    collapse of, 83
    important events in, **6–7**
    influence of, 11
    maximum size of, 8, **10**
Romanization, of conquered
    enemies, 51–52
Roman legions
    fighting techniques of,
        47–49
    medicine in, 44, 46
    requirements of recruits in,
        40–41

role in Romanizing enemies,
    50–52, 55
size of, 40
Romulus, 40

sacrificial rituals, 74
Saturnalia (festival), 80–81, 82–83
secutor (gladiator), 66–67
Segetia (deity), 72
senators, 37
Seneca, 12, 21, 33
sharecroppers, 28
Shelton, Jo-Ann, 74–75, 76
shops, 34–35
slavery/slaves, 10–11, 27, **29**
    city, 32, 34
    farm, treatment of, 30–31
    Seneca on, 33
soothsayers (augers), 72, 74
Soranus of Ephesus, 13
Statius, 58
subuclae (woolen vests), 53

Tacitus (historian), 41, 68
    on death of Vitellius, 74
    on Great Fire of Rome, 17
Tacitus (soldier), 53
temples, 75
Theodosius I (emperor), 82
thermae. See public baths
Timgad (military outpost), 57
togas, 22
Toner, J.P., 57
towns, 8–9

Trajan (emperor), 59, 60
tunics, 21–22

vastatio (war tactic), 50
Vegetius, Flavius, 43, 45
Venus (deity), 70
Vesta (deity), 79, 80
vestal virgins, **79,** 79–80
Vindolanda tablets, 53, 55

Vitellius (emperor), 74
Vitruvius (writer), 18

weapons, 49–50
women
    clothing/cosmetics of, 24–25
    economic role of, 38

Yegül, Fikret, 58

Picture Credits

Cover: © Stefano Bianchetti/Corbis

© Atlantide Phototravel/Corbis: 58

© Bettmann/Corbis: 42, 51, 61

© Stefano Bianchetti/Corbis: 20, 82

© Araldo de Luca/Corbis: 14, 71

© National Geographic Society/Corbis: 29

© Alfredo Dagli Orti/The Art Archive/Corbis: 67

Thinkstock Images: 6, 7, 36, 54

© Sandro Vannini/Corbis: 79

Steve Zmina: 10

Women's toilette in ancient Rome, Scarpelli, Tancredi (1866-19370/ Private Collection/© Look and Learn/The Bridgman Art Library: 24

About the Author

Stuart A. Kallen is the author of more than 250 nonfiction books for children and young adults. He has written on topics ranging from the theory of relativity to the history of rock and roll. In addition, Mr. Kallen has written award-winning children's videos and television scripts. In his spare time, he is a singer/songwriter/guitarist in San Diego.